# THE ALCHEMIST EXPOSED

# The
# Alchemist
## Exposed

by Robert Butler

NT  ⓑ

Published in 2006 by the National Theatre
in association with Oberon Books Ltd

National Theatre, South Bank, London SE1 9PX
www.nationaltheatre.org.uk/publications

Oberon Books
521 Caledonian Road, London N7 9RH
info@oberonbooks.com
www.oberonbooks.com

ISBN 978-1-84002-683-2

Photographs by Stephen Cummiskey

Cover design by Lisa Johnson, photograph of Alex Jennings and Simon Russell
Beale by Jillian Edelstein

Back cover photograph of Alex Jennings, Simon Russell Beale and Lesley
Manville in rehearsal by Stephen Cummiskey

Other books in the 'National Theatre at Work' series are: Robert Butler's
*Humble Beginnings*, *Just About Anything Goes*, and *The Art of Darkness*;
Jonathan Croall's *Hamlet Observed*, *Inside the Molly House*, and *Peter
Hall's Bacchai*; and Bella Merlin's *With the Rogue's Company*. Di Trevis'
*Remembrance of Things Proust* also explores the process of putting on a play
at the National.

Series editor Lyn Haill

Series © The National Theatre 2006

*Con artist Roy (Nicolas Cage) gives his 14-year-old daughter, Angela (Alison Lohman), her first lesson in the art of the con:*

## ROY

OK, the most important thing you have to understand about this game is, ninety per cent of it is variable. No matter how good your plan is you almost always get thrown a curve ball. So you got to be flexible, prepared to roll with anything. The one thing you can control, though, is who your mark is. Now, never play somebody who isn't buying what you're selling. You're thinking, "Daddy, Daddy, what am I selling?" Well, what you're selling is you.

*Matchstick Men*
screenplay by Nicholas Griffin & Ted Griffin

# Contents

# 1. 400 years in five minutes

YOU CAN LEAVE THE FOYER of the National Theatre, turn right, walk along the South Bank towards Blackfriars Bridge, and within a few minutes, you are at the site where Ben Jonson's *The Alchemist* had its first London performance, and where the action of the play is set. A five-minute walk from there takes you to the Temple Church, where two of the characters have a rendez-vous. (The same Temple Church figures in *The Da Vinci Code*.) A further five minutes brings you to Charing Cross, where Ben Jonson lived as a child. A few more minutes and you reach Westminster School, which Jonson attended, and next door to the school is Westminster Abbey where, 50 years later, he was buried.

It is all here: the names, places, some of the very same institutions; and yet it isn't. The tombstone and the play survive, along with a pile of other plays, several hundred pages of poetry and some portraits. But so much has happened in the 400 years between then and now that the world of Jacobean England is, in other respects, almost impossibly remote.

Thank God, you might think; life then was very harsh. When Ben Jonson was born, in 1572, he would have had a 50:50 chance of reaching the age of five. Someone from a poor background, like Jonson's, would have exceeded his life expectancy by the age of 26. Anyone who reached 40, which Jonson did two years after writing *The Alchemist*, was considered to have entered the first stage of old age.

The single biggest difference between then and now was the constant threat of death. London was repeatedly struck by bubonic plague. The first sign was a soft black swelling in the neck, groin or armpit. If you discovered that, you – and probably the rest of your family – would be dead within a week. (It killed two-thirds of those infected.) We now know what it was that was killing them and how to prevent it. They didn't. They put their faith in leaving town or sniffing sweet-smelling herbs.

Across Europe, religious tensions were leading to shocking acts of violence. The year Jonson was born, 3,000 Protestants were killed in Paris in the St Bartholomew's Day Massacre (and thousands more across France). As Jonson grew up there was the constant threat of Catholic insurrection or a Spanish invasion. When he was 15, the

Queen's Catholic cousin was executed. A year later, 130 Spanish ships set sail for England with 2,000 cannon and 20,000 men. Five years after his death, religious tensions would plunge England into civil war.

It was dangerous, but exciting. "England was full of newness and potential," writes Adam Nicolson in *Power and Glory*, "its population burgeoning, its merchant fleets combing the world, London growing like a hothouse plum, the sons of gentlemen crowding as never before into the colleges of Oxford and Cambridge, plants and fruits from all over the world arriving in its gardens and on its tables". Even the business of writing plays was a brand new career.

*The Alchemist* is a play about getting rich quick. Three con artists are coming up with every scheme they possibly can to separate people from their money. The alchemist in the play is a complete fraud and he and his two accomplices are pulling an elaborate scam known today as the *big con*, or *long con*. But alchemy itself is the search for the elixir, or the Philosopher's Stone, which would turn base metals into gold. It was taken very seriously by intelligent, educated people; it was a kind of science. The world of alchemists, Puritans and the plague seems hard to imagine.

Glance at the first couple of pages of *The Alchemist* and words like "kibes", "cozening" and "Christmas vails" leap out, which the footnotes explain are "chilblains", "cheating" and "Christmas tips". But it isn't possible to watch a play and follow the footnotes. When it opened, *The Alchemist* was a topical play and the audience would have understood the references. Four hundred years later, an audience might well say, "Sorry, this is too much like hard work."

Maybe a director should forget the Jacobean stuff, set the story in the present day and change any of the words that might confuse people. After all, as Hollywood proves year after year, everyone loves a story about a bunch of con artists. But then there might be little point in doing the play at all. Better to do something new. The person to ask was the director. Had *The Alchemist* passed its sell-by date? He was the one who had chosen to do it. He must know.

# 2. The Zammo test

EARLY JUNE: a month before rehearsals began, I went to see the play's director Nicholas Hytner in his office at the National Theatre, which overlooks the Thames (he can see Blackfriars from his window). Hytner is Director of the National Theatre and director of *The Alchemist*, so on this production, as with every other he directs here, he is director and producer.

He was director and producer of Philip Pullman's *His Dark Materials*, in which he found a way of staging daemons and parallel universes, Alan Bennett's *The History Boys*, which won six Tony awards on Broadway, Shakespeare's *Henry IV Parts 1 and 2*, and David Hare's *Stuff Happens*, about the politics that led to the war in Iraq.

The first thing Hytner did when I entered his office was hand me a new version of the script. The front cover said "*The Alchemist* by Ben Jonson." This was in large type in the centre of the page. In very small type, in the bottom left hand corner of the page, were the words: "Working draft inclusive of workshop edits 1st June 2006."

Rewrites are very common with new plays, but here was a 'working draft' of a play that had been around for centuries. Perhaps the older a play gets, the more drafts it requires. This new script had been produced by the playwright Samuel Adamson and was based on a workshop that had been held at the National Theatre Studio, when a number of actors had met with Hytner and Adamson and gone through the original text. Hytner began by explaining what they had done.

**NH** About 700 lines have been cut. We spent four days at the National Theatre Studio. We both had a bit of a go at it, but Sam in particular did some very subtle rewrites, where it is opaque. I don't think anyone will notice, except for the academics.

**RB** Will you be doing *The Alchemist* as if it took place in 1610?

**NH** With a fairly light touch, so that it has a foot in the contemporary world as well. Not unlike the approach I took on the two *Henry IVs*. *Henry IV* is rooted in three periods. It's rooted in the medieval world, it's rooted in their world [the Elizabethan world] and in our world. But I think the important thing is that you don't get hung up on Jacobean behaviour. The physical detail of the world is so Jacobean and so precise, and that makes it very very hard to do a comprehensive update. But you still want it to feel like it's a contemporary scam. I would like them to behave in a contemporary fashion and not have to invent some approximation, for instance, of Jacobean physical behaviour. It makes a huge difference if you don't have to think about something as banal as a hat.

**RB** It's not going to be presented as an exotic world, then, as a very different world?

**NH** It's different and exotic only to the extent that it needs to be and that it is fascinating. Something I'm personally not crazy about, and haven't done for ages and ages, is pick a period in the past that appears to have some kind of fit and then shove the play into that period. It did cross my mind – it was a purely opportunistic and rootless intuition – that it was kind of post-war, Francis Bacon Soho, and it would have the look of a post-war black and white English movie, with the grit of *Room at the Top*. It feels like one of the sharper Ealing comedies. It's in a tradition of English satirical humour, at the beginning of a tradition of English comedy – the English satirical scam. You could imagine it as one of those English gangster flicks. I hope that connection can be made just because it acts as a bridge. It would certainly solve some problems to update it, but it might create more problems than it would solve. I just keep running up against how much of it refers to a different world and how much of it is about that world. There are certain plays you can watch and carry in your head, simultaneously, the world it refers to, and the world that they chose to set it in. If you update *Julius Caesar*, nobody thinks that literally they're watching Blair and Bush or whatever, they know they're watching Julius Caesar, Brutus and Cassius.

**RB** An audience can hang on to the two ideas at the same time.

**NH** Yes. It's set in a contemporary world because a contemporary world and it seemed to spark so well together. I don't think the point of *Julius Caesar* is "1599" or "Rome", it's about men of power. Whereas, I think, with *The Alchemist*, part of the point is the world they live in.

**RB** The world of 1610, the plague the year before –

**NH** Yes, but it's not going to be a big period recreation at all. The clothes will sit easily in that period, but feel relaxed, have a kind of contemporary looseness. The set is an archetypal London house of any period.

**RB** You are always having to negotiate, I suppose, between the period when it was written and what an audience responds to today.

**NH** That is one of the jobs you have to do. And if that negotiation is helped by an update, you do the update. If it is hindered by the update, then you don't. I think the modern world is totally up for get-rich-quick stories and barking mad people and alchemistic equivalents.

**RB** Do you think Ben Jonson is reaching a point where he is almost becoming inaccessible?

**NH** I do. I'm afraid I think Shakespeare is. Unmediated or untranslated Shakespeare. 150 years: how long will it be? It will be an educational issue. We like to think that language doesn't develop, but we know it does. In 150 years, will it still be possible to do Shakespeare? I really don't know. Will it feel as remote as Chaucer does to us?

**RB** If you're an A-level English teacher, you want to teach Arthur Miller really. Because students get it.

**NH** And they do. At History A-level they don't teach the Reformation. They teach the rise of fascism.

**RB** Isn't setting it in 1610 going to distance an audience even further from the play?

**NH** Sometimes it's the best way, but the audience can be made to feel terribly remote. I'm going to do a Restoration comedy next – *The Man of Mode*. I will do it absolutely parallel with today, and that's why I'm doing it. Because reading it, I thought its concerns are precisely the concerns of idle, moneyed young people today, who are interested in money and sex. The fact that they get carried around in sedan chairs is neither here nor there. It really isn't about that. It's about people who fuck around.

**RB** So the realism is psychological.

**NH** Yes.

**RB** And the rest is lightly touched in.

**NH** If the dislocate is too great, then it doesn't work. *The Alchemist* is interesting because the basic plot, the basic scam, seems so familiar. A trite little formula I've used is that you do old plays for two reasons: to see how different things were and to see that they never change. The two run parallel, and you have to negotiate the relationship between those two every time.

**RB** I saw *The Merry Wives of Windsor* once in India. The idea of the young girl with the dowry. The audience got it completely.

**NH** I bet.

**RB** But Ben Jonson's world is very removed from our own. He was classically educated. He spoke Latin at school.

**NH** It is one of the reasons why his language is more remote than Shakespeare's. You can tell that there are certain grammatical patterns which are Latin ones. It doesn't have either the grace or the ease of Shakespeare. But it's wonderful stuff. It needs really good actors. Do you know the cast?

**RB** Alex Jennings, Simon Russell Beale –

**NH** Alex Jennings, Simon Russell Beale, Ian Richardson. Lesley Manville as Dol Common. I can stand back and light the blue touch paper. I can't wait. It will still need really driving. I think it has to go very very fast.

**RB** Do you think the audience is going to need any help in understanding the period?

**NH** We were thinking that Sam would write a prologue in which Alex or Simon would come on and say these are the things that you need to know. When we were doing the week at the Studio, we just read the play and put our hands up when we didn't understand it and asked ourselves, "Would it be useful to have a look at this line?" Much less needed tinkering with than I predicted. But I just thought, I wonder whether this is the future? Nobody goes to Shakespeare's history plays anymore knowing what they used to. Or rather fewer and fewer people. Take *Henry IV*. Fewer and fewer people even knew that we were dealing here with a king who had had the last king murdered. I think we probably won't do a prologue in the end, but you never know.

**RB** What kind of things would it say?

**NH** Stuff like: a quick run-down on alchemy, quick run-down on Philosopher's Stone, quick run-down on Puritanism, oh, and by the way, tobacco was the new drug. I could imagine sitting there and thinking, I'm really glad I know this and I'm being told this. On the other hand, I can't quite hear the tone of voice of this prologue. I think it could be a little arch.

**RB** Didn't Alan Bennett, at one stage, want to give a talk before the performances of *Madness of George III* so that he could explain the historical context?

**NH** Yes. You can't count on very much anymore. Did you see *Market Boy*? There's one bit where a couple of the young traders are trying to persuade the boy at the centre to do acid and he's resisting, and others are saying, "Don't do it! Don't do it!" and one of them says, "Remember Zammo!" and that's a big laugh, and I dutifully laugh every time. But I had to go to Google and find out who this Zammo is. It turns out he was a character on *Grange Hill* who very famously became a heroin junkie. I didn't know! Now I know! Now I sit laughing uproariously and looking in scorn at all the older people who look confused because they don't know who Zammo is. *Grange Hill* passed me by. I was too old for *Grange Hill*.

# 3. Don't google Ben Jonson – it's all here

IN THE MOVIE, *Heist*, the con artist and master cracksman, Joe Moore, is about to go on a dangerous trip. As he walks towards the car, his wife warns: "Stay in the shadows." He says: "Hey, everyone's going to be looking in the shadows." She asks: "Where's the place to be?" He replies: "The place to be is in the sun."

Our minds are naturally drawn towards the half-hidden, the overheard and whatever it was that was disappearing round the corner. The best con artists, like the best writers, are expert in controlling the flow of information, giving us just as much as we need, and allowing our over-active imaginations to fill in the rest. This is why you don't have to be stupid to be a *mark*. The more intelligent someone is, the easier it can be to deceive them. One of the essential skills in influencing other people's thoughts is to allow the crucial information (the *hook*) to appear as if it was not really supposed to have been heard at all.

The advertising guru David Ogilvy once said that no one wants to see an advertisement that says 'Advertisement'. The skill is an old one: it is making the mark or the audience voluntarily (or, even better, involuntarily) do the work. Ben Jonson wrote the first great play in the English language about con artists. There's no doubt he knew his subject. He had been in and out of jail. He had spent his life moving between the sun and the shadows.

It's been said that if it wasn't for Shakespeare, Jonson would be our national playwright and his greatest misfortune was to have had Shakespeare as a contemporary. This would have been news to him. When he died he was the most celebrated poet of his age and he went to his grave knowing people thought he was a better poet and a better playwright than Shakespeare.

Jonson had grown up in a village called Charing Cross, about a mile to the west of the city of London. His clergyman father had died a month before Jonson was born (in 1572) and, soon after that, his mother married a bricklayer. He went to a local elementary school near "the Bermudas", a warren of alleyways notorious for prostitution and crime. The one reference Jonson made to his first seven years was that he was "brought up poorly".

His circumstances changed, dramatically, when a friend of the family's, possibly the lawyer John Hoskyns or the antiquarian William Camden, paid for Jonson to go to Westminster, the most famous school in the land. The 120 boys at Westminster were up at five in the morning for a day's timetable that was devoted to lessons and prayers. Pupils were expected to speak Latin throughout the day (no English allowed) and by the time Jonson left he had received the firmest possible grounding in Greek and Latin literature, and performed in a number of classical plays. He couldn't afford to go to Cambridge (where he had a place) and went to work for his stepfather as a bricklayer, which he "could not endure".

Several details stand out that must have marked Jonson as a writer. One, he had no father. Two, his mother remarried and transferred her attention to another man. Three, he was a poor boy who went to the top school in the country. What quickly emerges, in any account of Jonson's life, is that he grew up in a world of extremes and had the personality to match it: his volcanic, unruly nature contended with a scholar's desire for precision.

Like many teenagers stuck in dead-end jobs, he threw it over and went abroad: joining the English army in the Netherlands, where he fought for the Dutch against the Spanish. One biographer, David Riggs, says he bore "a heavy load of resentment". Jonson went out of his way to prove himself by killing a man in single combat in view of both camps and, in the classical tradition, claiming the victor's spoils. After that, he returned to England.

For an aspiring playwright, he had chosen a bad moment to enter showbusiness. The plague had hit London badly between 1592 and 1594 and the theatres were closed for two years. This was just the time that Shakespeare, eight years his senior, was getting going as a playwright. He had written *Richard III* and *The Two Gentlemen of Verona* and, immediately after the two-year ban was lifted, he would write *The Comedy of Errors*, *The Taming of the Shrew* and *Love's Labour's Lost*.

In 1594, Jonson married Anne Lewis whom he later described to a friend as "a shrew yet honest". They soon had a daughter (who died at six months) and a son. The scholar Anne Barton writes that "Jonson was considerably more interested in other men's wives than in his own". Jonson's friend, the poet William Drummond, says the same: "he thought the use of a maid nothing in comparison to the wantonness of a wife and would never have any other mistress".

He joined a touring company of actors, where his classical education, formidable memory and skill as a swordsman would have been obvious assets. "All that the fledgling actor lacked," writes Riggs, "was talent." Jonson was back in London by 1597 and got work in July as an actor, and then as a playwright, from the theatre manager, Philip Henslowe. It was a good moment for a writer with Jonson's sardonic cast of mind as there was a fashion for satire. Two years later Shakespeare would catch this scornful mood in *As You Like It* when Jaques says:

Give me leave
To speak my mind, and I will through and through
Cleanse the foul body of th'infected world  (II.vii)

But Jonson overdid it (he often did). His first play, *Isle of Dogs*, which he co-wrote with an old rival Thomas Nashe, hasn't survived, but it was sufficiently scandalous for Jonson to be charged with "lewd and mutinous behaviour". The results won Jonson few friends in the theatre. The Lord Mayor ordered not only the closure but the demolition of the playhouses, including (he named the actual venues) the Theatre and the Curtain. Nashe fled London, but Jonson went to Marshalsea prison that summer, where he found himself "in close imprisonment," observed by two of the most sinister figures in Elizabethan England, the government torturer Richard Topcliffe and the charismatic spy Robert Poley.

Jonson's fortunes picked up the next year when his play *Every Man In His Humour* was performed by the Lord Chamberlain's Men, with a main role played by William Shakespeare. This was the first version of the play: later he would relocate the action from Florence to London. It was probably also in 1598 that the Children of the Chapel Royal performed *The Case is Altered*, based on plays by Plautus, which has at its centre a father who has lost two sons, and who (by the end of the play) will have both of them restored to him.

But disaster struck again. Jonson got into an argument with another actor in Henslowe's company, fought him in a duel and killed him. He was tried at the Old Bailey and imprisoned in Newgate. While he was in prison, he converted (illegally) to Roman Catholicism, which may have allowed him – as he faced the death penalty – to receive a degree of absolution that would have been unavailable from an Anglican priest.

Jonson escaped the death penalty by pleading 'benefit of clergy', an old law allowing clemency to those who could read the so-called 'neck-verse' from the Bible (Psalm 51:1). All his goods were confiscated (he had a wife and family to support), and his thumb was branded with the letter 'T' for Tyburn, the place where he would have been executed.

He was not an easy man to have in a theatre company. His first play had resulted in orders to shut down the theatres themselves. When he rejoined the company he killed one of the other actors. The only thing going for him was that he could write. *Every Man In His Humour* must have been very good box office because the next year he wrote *Every Man Out Of His Humour* and it was put on at the new Globe theatre.

He was also writing for children: between 1600 and 1601 he wrote *Cynthia's Revels* and *Poetaster*, performed by Children of the Chapel Royal. It was during this period Jonson became embroiled in a series of literary skirmishes that became known as "The War of the Theatres". Jonson had been upset by John Marston's portrait of him as a philosopher in *Histriomastix* and retaliated by satirising Marston in *Every Man Out Of His Humour*. Marston hit back at Jonson's retaliation with another portrait of Jonson in *Jack Drum's Entertainment*.

The war then moved on to another, more sophisticated, level with Jonson portraying himself as the Roman poet Horace in *Poetaster* and (as Horace) satirising Marston and Thomas Dekker. The prolific Dekker, who wrote *The Shoemakers' Holiday*, probably joined forces with Marston on *Satiromastix* to portray Horace, and therefore Jonson, as a self-promoter, flicking "ink in every man's face". The notoriety caused by this in-fighting may have helped Jonson's finances. In 1602 he had been paid two pounds by Henslowe to write some additions to Thomas Kyd's *Spanish Tragedy*. The next year he was paid £10 by Henslowe for further additions and a new script.

Queen Elizabeth died in 1603 and James I ascended the throne. It was also the year when the plague struck again, this time claiming 30,000 lives. For Jonson, it was a terrible year professionally and personally. His play *Sejanus* flopped (Shakespeare, again, was in the cast). Far worse, one of the victims of the plague was his seven-year-old son Benjamin. In a poem titled 'On My First Son', Jonson writes:

Farewell, thou child of my right hand, and joy;
My sin was too much hope of thee, loved boy.

He describes his son as his "best piece of poetry".

Two years later another play landed him in jail. Jonson co-wrote *Eastward Ho!* with George Chapman and his old adversary,

John Marston. The three of them were arrested for the play's anti-Scots jokes (the King, of course, was a Scot). The actual lines that provoked the arrest hadn't been written by Jonson, but he voluntarily accompanied his colleagues to prison. So far his career as a playwright had been chiefly distinguished by two decent comedies, a number of flops, some literary in-fighting, the death of a fellow actor and some dangerous spells in prison. It was hard to see how he was about to rival Shakespeare.

And yet, over the next five years, the careers of two of the world's greatest dramatists would shadow one another as they produced a series of plays that have been performed ever since. In 1606 Shakespeare wrote *Macbeth*, in 1607 he wrote *Antony and Cleopatra* and in 1610 he wrote *The Winter's Tale*. In 1606, Jonson wrote his first comic masterpiece, *Volpone*. In 1610 he wrote his second, *The Alchemist*.

# 4. Things are not as they seem

IT WAS THE CITY OF SCAM. The *gull* could be visiting a well-known tourist site in London – St Paul's Cathedral, for instance – and suddenly a man faints and hits the floor. The gull goes over to help, the man recovers, thanks him and leaves. Later that day the gull can't find his money. Another time he hears a man announce there are pickpockets operating in the area. Very discreetly, he checks he still has his money on him. A second pickpocket, working with the man making the announcement, watches to see exactly where the gull's hand has gone. Or, more embarrassingly, the gull visits a prostitute and (halfway through) a man storms in, says he is the woman's husband, gets very angry and exacts compensation.

These were three of the most obvious ways of getting conned in Jacobean London and they still work today. Cheating with dice and cards were two others: card-players staged games with accomplices winning high stakes to lure in gulls. Dice men drew on 14 kinds of false dice (as well as sleight of hand) to roll the right numbers. A rash of pamphlets appeared during Ben Jonson's childhood warning visitors to the city – particularly young 'greenhorns' up from the country – about the hazards they faced. But for newcomers it was an unequal struggle.

It might have been Chicago in the Twenties or Moscow in the Nineties. "The London underworld was highly organised," writes the literary scholar Gāmini Salgādo, "far more efficiently organised, indeed, than the forces of law and order." Criminals developed very specific skills, organised rapid disposal of goods and diligently trained young recruits. The Artful Dodger was alive and well 250 years before Charles Dickens sat down and invented him.

In the *short con*, the gull – or *mark*, as he became known – is fleeced of the money he has on him; in the *big con* he is sent home to get more. Con artists have many sayings, and the most important one is "you can't cheat an honest man". The key ingredient for the big con is the complicity of the victim. The mark has to be tempted into joining a shady get-rich-quick scheme that requires money upfront. The main scams in *The Alchemist* closely follow the same routines that David Maurer observed in *The Big Con* (1940), his classic account of American confidence men between 1900 and 1920, when cities like

Chicago, Miami and Atlanta were expanding as rapidly as London had been in 1610.

In *The Alchemist* we see a bogus naval captain, Face, a bogus alchemist, Subtle, and a bogus aristocratic lady, Dol Common, working several versions of the big con. It always starts, to use the American jargon, with the *roper* going out, finding the mark and winning his trust. (This is Face's job.) The *roper* then introduces the mark to the *insideman*, who has some special knowledge to share. (This is Subtle's role.) The roper always pretends to be on the side of the mark and together they hear from the insideman how the mark is going to get rich. American con men call this *telling the tale*.

Once the mark has been convinced by the scheme he is sent home to get as much money as he can. (The phrase for this is *putting him on the send*.) When the mark returns, the roper and the insideman fleece him of all his money (*taking off the touch*). After that, they have to make sure the mark leaves as quickly and quietly as possible (*blowing him off*). Very few con artists are arrested or prosecuted. Once the mark has lost his money, complicity turns to shame or embarrassment, and he is reluctant to tell either the police or his friends.

The great majority of today's scams operate through the internet with its limitless opportunities for identity and password theft, the offering of bargain basement deals (especially low fare travel) that have to be purchased today, and the dozens of variations on the 'Nigerian Letter' – so-called because of the widespread occurrence of the scam in Nigeria. The letter used to be sent by fax; today, an email arrives from someone wanting to transfer a large amount of money out of one country and into another, and offering the person who helps with the transfer a sizeable cut. All the person needs to do is contribute towards some small logistical payments that need to be met along the way.

Few of the 21st-century scams have the style of a con artist like Victor Lustig who managed to sell off the Eiffel Tower. In 1925 he posed as deputy director-general of the French Ministry of Posts and Telegraphs and set up private meetings with six scrap-metal dealers. He said the matter was highly sensitive (if news leaked, there would be a public outcry) and negotiations had to be conducted in strictest secrecy. He met the merchants at the impeccably grand Hotel de Crillon, in the Place de la Concorde, where he explained that the government had decided the expense of maintaining the Eiffel Tower was too high and was going to sell it off as scrap metal. It was his job to invite confidential bids from the merchants. Lustig had rented a limousine and took the merchants on a tour of the Eiffel Tower. Eventually, he awarded the non-existent contract to the one man who was also prepared to bribe him. Lustig got away with the money and the bribe.

It is hard not to applaud when con artists behave as the aristocrats of crime. In his essay on 'Diddling', the American short story writer Edgar Allan Poe listed their qualities as "minuteness, interest, perseverance, ingenuity, audacity, nonchalance, originality, impertinence, and grin". There is an enormous gulf between the mugger, for instance, who is guilty of theft and violence (or threats of violence), and the con artist, who considers himself not guilty on any of those counts.

"Although the confidence man is sometimes classed with professional thieves, pickpockets and gamblers," writes Maurer in *The Big Con*, "he is really not a thief at all because he does no actual stealing. The trusting victim literally thrusts a fat bankroll into his hands. It is a point of pride with him that he does not have to steal."

Playwrights and screenwriters have always loved con artists. Maurer gives a scholarly account of a Big Store con, where a fake bookmaker is set up with fake customers and fake bets and the local wire service (also fake) delays the racing results. It was the inspiration for the film *The Sting* (1973), which went on to win seven Academy Awards. But tricksters, cozeners and cony-catchers have provided mainstream entertainment since classical times. There is a rich vein running through Jonson, who knew his Latin playwrights, to Tobias Smollett, Daniel Defoe and Herman Melville, who wrote *The Confidence Man*. In the movies it stretches from the sophisticated wit of Preston Sturges' *The Lady Eve* to the glossy panache of Steven Soderbergh's remake of *Ocean's Eleven*.

The most thoughtful modern exponent of the genre is David Mamet. "Drama is basically about lies," he told an interviewer, "somebody lying to somebody". In movies like *House of Games*, *The Spanish Prisoner* and *Heist* he plays with ideas of trust and betrayal and the illusionist's ability to steer the mind of the mark (and therefore the audience) in the wrong direction. In this world of 'autosuggestion' the con artist emerges as an expert in cognitive behaviour.

"I gave you my trust," says the indignant psychiatrist Margaret (Lindsay Crouse) at the end of *House of Games*. "Of course you gave me your trust," replies the con artist Mike (Joe Mantegna), who has tricked her out of $80,000, "That's what I do for a living. You asked me what I did for a living. This is it."

The prolific American crime writer Jim Thompson was taught how to palm $10 and $20 bills when he worked as a bell-hop in a Texan hotel. The technique he learnt in the 1920s was the same technique he gave his central character, Roy Dillon, in *The Grifters*. (He was played by John Cusack in the movie.) Thompson makes the job of the con sound very close to his own. "There are thirty-two ways to write a story," he said, "and I've used every one, but there is only one plot – *things are not as they seem*."

# 5. Seven plots on the go

AT ANY ONE MOMENT, hundreds of Hollywood writers are trying to come up with the perfect plot and there are dozens of books available to explain what exactly is required: 'inciting incidents', 'hero's journey', 'reversals', 'character arcs', 'the counter-idea', 'deep character', 'obligatory scenes'; the list goes on and on. Well, in 1610 Ben Jonson came up with one. It is almost official. The great English poet, Samuel Taylor Coleridge, said *The Alchemist* had one of the three perfect plots. He said the other two were *Oedipus Rex* by Sophocles, which was written around about 430BC, and *Tom Jones* by Henry Fielding, which was written in 1749. That's three in 2,000 years: quite a low strike rate.

This particular perfect plot takes place in one location within a period of about six hours and interweaves seven separate storylines. If Jonson had been a Hollywood screenwriter he would probably have stuck a large chart up on a wall, with each of the seven storylines represented by a different colour and all the places marked where the stories intersected. It would look like a map of the London Underground. Only easier to get lost in.

There are three main reasons why *The Alchemist* can be hard to follow. The first is the language. Jonson was very erudite and didn't mind sharing his learning with others. The second is that the opening scene is a furious argument between the three con artists during which we learn how it is that they got to be where they are now. (If you can't follow that bit, and they often take it fast and loud, you've had it.) The third is that the central characters spend a lot of time pretending to be other people.

Imagine there was a clock on the wall of the house where the con artists are operating: the events in *The Alchemist* would happen between about nine in the morning and three in the afternoon. But the whole story, everything you need to understand for it to fall into place, goes back over a couple of months. For the purposes of understanding that plot, it is necessary to go back to the day the master left the house.

The story of *The Alchemist* begins when an elderly widower, Lovewit, leaves his town house in Blackfriars, in the City of London, to escape the threat of the plague. He takes nearly all of his possessions with him and heads off for his country estate, probably in Kent, where he grows hops. He leaves a single servant to look after the house, a caretaker really, whose name is Jeremy.

After his boss has gone, Jeremy goes to Pie Corner in Smithfield, well-known for its food stalls, where he meets a man who is down on his luck. A scrawnier individual would be hard to imagine: he wears rags, mouldy slippers, and a thin, threadbare cloak that barely covers his almost non-existent buttocks. He is so poor he can't afford any food and hovers round the stalls feeding off the steam. He doesn't even have the money or possessions to light a fire to warm himself. This is the con artist, Subtle.

The two of them get talking and hit on an idea for a scam. Con artists either use real-life settings, which is called *playing a man against a wall*, or they create fake settings, like the Big Store con, where a venue is fitted out to look like a real shop or bookmaker's. (This is what they do in *The Sting*.) In con terms, the pair decide on a plan that is halfway between the two. They are going to take over Lovewit's house in Blackfriars and pretend that Subtle is an alchemist, and that there is another room in the house that is a fully equipped laboratory, where tremendous experiments are taking place, and where – one day soon! – they will produce the Philosopher's Stone, the secret elixir, the liquid that will transmute base metals into gold.

Jeremy provides Subtle with a venue, which he can pass off as his own house, and gives him some money to buy enough equipment to give the impression that experiments are taking place in the other room. But Subtle believes that it is *he* who is doing Jeremy the favour. If Jeremy were left to his own devices, he imagines, he would end up on his own in a dark and dingy pub. Thanks to Subtle, he can say goodbye to the tedium of life as a modest servant, busying himself with brooms, dust and watering-pots. Thanks to Subtle, he will become an assistant in the great and ancient art of alchemy. Subtle's first job is to give him a makeover. The lowly butler Jeremy will be turned into "Captain Face", a thoroughly respectable and decent chap. As Captain Face, as he now is, Jeremy will be sent out into the city to win people's trust.

Ben Jonson had a long experience of collaboration with other writers, actors and designers. He knew how hard it could be to work with people and share the credit (it was a major cause of his falling out with the designer Inigo Jones). The running sore that develops between Subtle and Face is a familiar one: who is doing the most work and who is more deserving of the reward? In con terms, Face is the *roper*, who brings in the *mark*, and Subtle is the *insideman* who does the razzle-dazzle, explaining to the mark how he can make lots of money. Subtle has the education to do the fancy alchemical talk, but as Face says, "You must have stuff brought home for you to work on."

In most big cons, which involve a sustained deception over days or weeks, other people are required to work as *extras* or *shills*. This job is taken by an associate of Subtle's, a prostitute called Dol Common. The three of them form a "venture tripartite", an agreement which says that the three of them are in this together, that they are all equal and that they will split the money three ways. The way Dol talks about the arrangement ("begun out of equality", "all things in common"), she might have done a degree in political theory. Face is not worried that his boss will make an unexpected return because he knows Lovewit is so fearful of the plague he won't come back to London until the death rate falls to almost zero. Lovewit has said that before he returns he will write to Jeremy with instructions to air the rooms.

Five or six weeks pass, and the scam is going very well. Face has grown a beard, and goes round the London pubs, drumming up business (*putting the mark up*). He meets people, he wins their trust, he finds out what their secret wishes are, and he tells them about this very successful alchemist he knows – or this fortune-teller, or this necromancer, or this conjuror – and he offers to go along and introduce them. The substantial house in Blackfriars is evidence itself of Subtle's high standing. Subtle passes himself off as whatever it is that Face has set him up to be. Sometimes Face changes his clothes and appears in the house as the bellows man, Ulen Spiegel, who assists Subtle in the laboratory. During these weeks, as more and more visitors come in and out of the house, the neighbours peep out of their windows (from behind lace curtains, if they have them) and wonder what is going on.

Like nearly all con artists, Subtle holds out the prospect of imminent wealth while asking for a modest investment in advance, and then – as the con deepens – the requests for money grow more urgent as the possibility of greater and greater riches seems to get tantalisingly close. If the con artist ever thinks the mark is losing interest he will put *the chill* on him, making out that he doesn't really think that he can continue with this project. This soon revives the mark's interest. The stage beyond that is the *tear-up*, when the con artist literally tears up the cheque, or hands back the money to the mark, to show that he is entirely trustworthy and disinterested.

The big con has been working well with Sir Epicure and, also, with members of the Anabaptist sect. A regular visitor, Sir Epicure believes he is about to become possessor of the Philosopher's Stone. Subtle has told him that they are nearing the very final stages of the alchemical process, the moment of 'projection', when the liquid reddens, shortly before it turns to gold. Sir Epicure has invested substantially in this project, giving Subtle £80 (big money: the annual salary of a schoolmaster was £15), but Sir Epicure is so confident that he is about to hit the jackpot that he is bringing along a friend of his, Pertinax Surly, a gambler, whom he is keen to impress. Surly is an experienced card player and thinks alchemy is a "pretty kind of game" – like card tricks, in fact – "to cheat a man, with charming".

With Sir Epicure, Subtle and Face are reaching a critical point in the life cycle of the con. They are approaching the moment when they must *take off the touch*, that is, get all the money they can out of him (and, if not money, any other goods). They will also need to *blow him off*. They need to create a situation in which everything goes wrong and in which Sir Epicure is clearly responsible for that turn of events. This is where Dol comes in.

Sir Epicure knows that to be a true alchemist, and have a shot at discovering the Philosopher's Stone, he would have to be a holy man with no impious thoughts. His solution has been to find a man who has the requisite holiness (he believes Subtle to be this person) and then buy the stone from him. For this final stage of the con to work, Dol will disguise herself as an alluring aristocratic lady and will tempt Sir Epicure into some kind of indiscretion. ("Why this is yet a kind of modern happiness," thinks Face, relishing the task, "to have Dol Common for a great lady.") The result? The atmosphere of holiness will be broken, the alchemical experiment will be wrecked and they will blame Sir Epicure. He will readily acknowledge his errors and they will kick him out of the house. All his money will be theirs.

Sir Epicure isn't the only one looking for a speedy recoupment of his financial outlay. The Anabaptists are also concerned that they had made a substantial investment for goods from Subtle without seeing any return. When the young deacon, Ananias, complains to Subtle about this, Subtle will pretend to lose his tempter and kick him out of the house. Ananias will have to return later, accompanied by a superior, Tribulation Wholesome, who will try to placate the great alchemist.

This morning two other young men are about to enter the Blackfriars house for the first time. One of the skills of a good roper is to draw in a mark who only has modest ambitions and then, when the roper has introduced the mark to the insideman, and the mark has been told the tale, the mark's ambitions become inflamed to a wild degree. This is what will happen to Dapper and Drugger.

Face only met the young clerk, Dapper, in a pub in Holborn the previous evening. As a clerk, Dapper's job is to copy out legal documents (there were no photocopiers then) and all he wants is a bit of luck at the races or when rolling dice. Some modest success might well impress the minor poets, one or two of whom he has met, and give him some independence from his grandmother.

But once Subtle gets hold of Dapper, the young man's ambition will begin to soar. Dapper will come to believe that he was born under a rare star, that the Queen of the Fairies presides over it, and that if he wants to meet the Queen of the Fairies he will have to undergo "a world of ceremonies". He will need to be bathed and fumigated, wear a clean shirt and prepare himself with drops of vinegar in his nose, mouth and ears. (All this he will do.) Dapper will then find himself dressed in a petticoat, blind-folded, pinched by the fairies and locked in a loo.

Face has also won the confidence of a young tobacconist, Abel Drugger, who is setting up a shop and wants advice on where to put the shelves, boxes, containers and door. ("All I want is to thrive.") Face has told Drugger that Subtle has special knowledge that will be of great help. When Drugger meets Subtle he will explain that "I was wished to your worship by a gentleman, one Captain Face, that says you know men's planets, and their good angels, and their bad." The roper always takes the side of the mark and so Face will vouch for Drugger, telling Subtle that he is an honest fellow (and no usurer) who provides him with decent tobacco. (Actually, Face thinks Drugger is miserable and has worms.)

Subtle will explain to Drugger that he works by 'metoposcopy' and 'chiromancy'; he studies the face and reads hands. He will give Drugger precise instructions about the layout of his shop ("make your door then, south") and will tell him there is even more good news if he is prepared to pay for it. One day, he believes, Drugger may become a great alchemist and even discover the Philosopher's Stone. Drugger will offer Subtle a crown for this amazing information and the offer will be treated with disdain (a crown was five shillings). Drugger will remember that he has a sovereign (a sovereign was 20 shillings) and will hand that over.

By the time he returns he will be so hooked that he will bring news of a young woman who lives near him – 19, rich and a widow – who has come to live in London and wants to have her fortune told. More than that, this widow has a brother who has just inherited £3,000 a year (the equivalent of millions today) and has come up from his country estate to learn how to quarrel like one of the fashionable young blades of London. Drugger will be sent away, this time to fetch Dame Pliant and her brother Kastril, and Face will suggest to the young tobacconist that Subtle may be able to arrange his marriage to the young widow.

This hectic morning, then, will see the arrival at the Blackfriars house of Dapper, Drugger, Sir Epicure, Surly and Ananias, and later, Tribulation and Dame Pliant and her brother, Kastril. Later still, there will be another, very unexpected visitor. But right now, a day's work lies ahead and the day has started badly. The three con artists are in violent disagreement. Subtle has a vial of chemical liquid in his hand which he is threatening to throw at Face and Face has drawn his sword and is threatening Subtle. At this very moment, the play begins.

# 6. One thing turns into another

A PLAY CAN HAVE MANY LIVES, as its subject matter resonates with a new audience, or as an actor comes along, seizes a role and transforms how the play is seen. Since its first performance *The Alchemist* has (like a good con artist) frequently shifted its identity.

*The Alchemist* didn't open in London as the theatres were still closed on account of the plague in 1609. It was performed for the very first time in Oxford in September 1610. There were no reviews of the Oxford production, but one member of the audience, a university don called Henry Jackson, recorded his reaction. He was appalled. Yes, he conceded, the actors received "very great applause". The problem was that "not content with attacking alchemists, they most foully violated the sacred scriptures themselves".

The date of the play's action is 1 November 1610, which may well be the date of the first London performance. Despite Henry Jackson's reservations, maybe even because of them, *The Alchemist* was popular during Jonson's lifetime and continued to be so during the Restoration. The diarist Samuel Pepys saw a performance in 1661 (22 June) and thought it "most incomparable".

*The Alchemist* enjoyed remarkable popularity during the 18th century. Between 1709 and 1776 it was in almost continuous production, becoming especially popular after an historic event in 1720. The South Sea Bubble was a get-rich-quick scheme on a massive scale; in Parliament alone, the feverish speculation, and rewards that rapidly accrued, attracted 462 MPs and 122 peers. When the Bubble burst, wrote Winston Churchill in his *A History of the English-Speaking Peoples*, "The porters and ladies' maids who had bought carriages and fineries found themselves reduced to their former station. Clergy, bishops, poets and gentry found their life savings vanish overnight." More than 100 years after *The Alchemist* was first performed, it had acquired a new relevance from an event that hadn't existed when it was written.

Even within the play, stock was rising and falling. There are 12 named roles in the play and one of them gradually took on a remarkable life of its own. This was the part of the tobacconist, Abel Drugger, who wants advice on the layout of his new shop. A series of actors triumphed in the role: the first to do so was William Pinkethman; he was succeeded by the farceur Theophilus Cibber. At one performance Cibber accidentally broke the urinal. The audience thought this so hilarious that breaking the urinal became an established part of the comic business of the play.

The greatest actor of the 18th century, David Garrick, opened in the role of Abel Drugger on 21 March 1743. He had cut the play's 3,000 lines down to 2,000. *The Alchemist* now ran just over two hours. Not surprisingly, Garrick placed most of the emphasis on the little tobacconist, even introducing new moments into the play. The 154 cuts included 250 lines from Sir Epicure's role and some of the ruder parts of the play, which he thought would offend the audience of his day. He knew his market. Garrick went on to produce the play once or twice a year for more than 30 years.

He also revolutionised acting by introducing a new naturalness. It was this that enabled him to distance his portrayal from the celebrated one given by Cibber, who had clearly been a bit of a ham. A contemporary account says that Cibber had "mixed so much absurd grimace and ridiculous tricks in playing this part, that although the galleries laughed and clapped their hands, the judicious part of the audience was displeased".

Garrick had the audacity to do as little as possible. "The moment he came upon the stage, he discovered such awkward simplicity, and his looks so happily bespoke the ignorant, selfish, and absurd tobacco-merchant, that it was a contest not easily to be decided, whether the burst of laughter or applause were loudest."

The performance was remarkably life-like. A grocer from Garrick's home town of Lichfield came to see the play bringing with him a letter of introduction from Garrick's brother, Peter. The grocer was so taken in by Garrick's performance that when he returned to Lichfield he confessed to Peter that he could not bring himself to hand over the letter. "Though he is your brother, Mr Garrick," he said, "he is one of the shabbiest, meanest, most pitiful hounds I ever saw in the whole course of my life."

Drugger's appeal as a character led to spin-offs and merchandise. One was the founding of a tobacco shop in London called 'The Abel Drugger'. The playwright Francis Gentleman wrote two plays that cashed in on the character's success. In the first one, *The Tobacconist*, he rewrites *The Alchemist* so that Drugger becomes its hero. In the second one, *The Pantheonites*, he moves the story forward in time and features the adventures of Dan Drugger, the great-grandson of Jonson's character.

Then *The Alchemist* disappears. Between the end of the 18th century and the end of the 19th, it falls out of the repertoire. (The spin-off did better: the great Shakespearean actor Edmund Kean appeared in *The Tobacconist* in 1815.) It was not until 1899 that the intrepid director William Poel revived the play for the Elizabethan Stage Society. It was performed at the Apothecaries' Hall, Blackfriars, the site of its first theatre.

After the Second World War, there was a star-studded revival with Ralph Richardson as Face, Margaret Leighton as Dame Pliant, and Alec Guinness as Abel Drugger. The critic Kenneth Tynan describes Guinness's performance as "the puny tobacconist…his wistful, happy eyes moving, in dumb wonder, from Face to Subtle". When Drugger manages momentarily to hold his own in conversation with Subtle and Face, "his face creases ruddily into modest delight, and he stamps his thin feet in glee". Tynan concluded: "Drugger used to be Garrick's part, but, Mr Guinness having now appropriated it, I name him the best living English character-actor."

The founder of Theatre Workshop, Joan Littlewood, staged the play in 1953, with near fatal results. Sir Epicure enters at the beginning of the second act, saying, "This is the day, wherein, to all my friends, I will pronounce the happy word, be rich." At that very moment, the iron safety curtain came crashing down onto the stage. The actor playing Surly swiftly stepped out of character to grab the actor playing Sir Epicure. The safety curtain, Littlewood later wrote, "would have killed him".

By the early 1960s, the play was 350 years old, which some people felt was very old indeed. The director Tyrone Guthrie had achieved a number of successes doing classic plays in modern dress, starting with a *Hamlet* with Alec Guinness in the lead. In 1962 he staged a modern dress version of *The Alchemist* at the Old Vic. This was a key moment in the play's history: could *The Alchemist* change into something as contemporary as The Beatles?

Guthrie argued in *The Times* that an update was essential as an audience did not know enough about the Jacobean age to understand Jonson's play in its original form. He also believed that modern dress gave more point to the disguises and impersonations used by the trio of rogues. In a programme note, Guthrie wrote: "In Jacobean dress, who would know when Face was a Captain or a House Servant? Whether Subtle was a Divine or a Doctor?"

The argument was vigorously attacked by Bamber Gascoigne in the *Spectator*. (The Zammo test, here: anyone over 40 will know Gascoigne as the crisp, benign quiz-master on *University Challenge*; he is also the author of a history of theatre.) Gascoigne found the production an "almost total disaster". In his review, he wrote: "There is an obvious case for anyone who wishes to rewrite such a play completely, turning it into a comedy which a twentieth-century Ben Jonson might have written. But this task does require a twentieth-century Ben Jonson."

Guthrie's modern dress version, he argued, fell precisely between two valid extremes. "He makes no change in the core of the play, in its plot or characterisation, but he plays merry havoc with the peripheral details." If an audience can make the connections in its own mind between a Jacobean con artist and a modern-day con artist, did "a coach and six" need to be rewritten as a "limousine"? Did Kastril need to wear black leather biker's gear and a crash helmet so that the Jacobean "angry boy" can be turned into a Sixties Teddy Boy?

"Of all Elizabethan or Jacobean dramatists," Gascoigne wrote, "Jonson is probably the one who will suffer most from the Guthrie treatment. *The Alchemist* contains many more precise references to contemporary life and manners than any of Shakespeare's plays, and also many more remarks about the precise appearance of other characters in the play." Gascoigne concluded, forcefully, "A play begins to be relevant when it is true in its own context. It becomes fully relevant when that truth holds good for other parallel contexts." Not everyone agreed: in his introduction to the Penguin edition of Jonson's *Three Comedies*, Michael Jamieson describes the Guthrie production as "fast and farcical and marvellously entertaining".

Anxieties about how to stage the play were deepening with the years. When director Peter Dews staged *The Alchemist* at Chichester in 1970 he threw in as many comic effects as he could manage. This dismayed the *Observer* critic Ronald Bryden, who wrote that the sheer number of "funny hats, funny voices, custard pies and chamber pots suggested a belief that the only way to deal with Jonson's rich, intricate verbal invention was to bury it under farcical hubbub". It looked as if *The Alchemist* had reached a point where people might be losing confidence in the play itself.

One playwright in particular, Peter Barnes, became a champion of Jonson's, calling for a wealthy patron to donate a Republican Jonson Theatre to rival the Royal Shakespeare Company. It would have to be republican, he argued, because "no kings or queens stalk through his pages". Jonson didn't give us rulers, Barnes wrote, he gave us "the ruled, and proves they are every bit as interesting and important".

In 1977 Barnes worked on a new version of *The Alchemist* for the RSC, which was directed by Trevor Nunn and starred Ian McKellen as Face. On his website, McKellen admits that he was appalled, on reading the original dialogue, "to discover how the verbose and often archaic lines masked the wit and basic humorousness of the characters". He was relieved that Barnes was there "to clarify lines and moments that, despite everyone's best intentions, might be lost". The drama critic Bernard Levin did not approve of these intentions and attacked the production on the grounds that he personally had no problem understanding Jonson.

Nicholas Hytner's production of *The Alchemist*, with Simon Russell Beale as Face, Alex Jennings as Subtle, and Ian Richardson as Sir Epicure Mammon, opened at the National Theatre in September 2006. It was part of the Travelex £10 Season in the Olivier, which meant that two-thirds of the audience could see the play for £10.

# 7. Rehearsals

## The Cast

| | |
|---|---|
| Subtle | Alex Jennings |
| Face | Simon Russell Beale |
| Dol Common | Lesley Manville |
| Dapper | Bryan Dick |
| Abel Drugger | Amit Shah |
| Sir Epicure Mammon | Ian Richardson |
| Pertinax Surly | Tim McMullan |
| Tribulation Wholesome | Ian Barritt |
| Ananias | Sam Spruell |
| Kastril | Tristan Beint |
| Dame Pliant | Elisabeth Dermot Walsh |
| Lovewit | John Burgess |
| Neighbours | Sarah Annis |
| | Natalie Best |
| | Jason Cheater |
| | Paul Chesterton |
| | John Cummins |
| | Simon Markey |
| | Andrew McDonald |

## The Creative Team

| | |
|---|---|
| Director | Nicholas Hytner |
| Designer | Mark Thompson |
| Lighting Designer | Mark Henderson |
| Music | Grant Olding |
| Sound Designer | Rich Walsh |
| Dialect Coach | Charmian Hoare |
| Company Voice Work | Kate Godfrey |

## The Production Team

| | |
|---|---|
| Production Manager | Sacha Milroy |
| Staff Director | Derek Bond |
| Stage Manager | Emma B Lloyd |
| Deputy Stage Manager | Anna Hill |
| Assistant Stage Managers | Brewyeen Rowland |
| | Matt Watkins |
| Costume Supervisor | Irene Bohan |
| Assistants to the Designer | Colin Falconer and Luis Carvalho |
| Assistant to the Lighting Designer | Beky Stoddart |
| Assistant Production Manager | Jo Peake |
| Design Associate | Nick Murray |
| Textual Adviser | Samuel Adamson |
| Production Photographer | Stephen Cummiskey |

# Day 1: Monday

MID JULY: on the first day of rehearsals the cast were told by the director that there was one reason why people were going to come and see *The Alchemist*. Hytner was winding up his opening speech to the company when he got to this bit. He had said that the play required very precise, high definition acting; that Jonson was like Charles Dickens in that he got completely high on the people he was mocking; and that it was a story about con men who turn in on themselves, like a lot of present-day movies really – in fact, it was the prototype for all those movies.

There wasn't a model of the set for the cast to look at today (the designer, Mark Thompson, would be joining them in a couple of days) but the object of the set design had not been to come up with a big statement about the play. The cast should imagine an archetypal Georgian house, in Spitalfields, for instance, before it was gentrified and became chic. The interior would have the feel of a waiting room, a collection of chairs, a coffee table, some magazines.

Hytner told the company that there wasn't going to be a read-through – the usual ordeal actors go through on the first morning, when they sit in a circle and read the whole play. He had directed *Volpone* 15 years ago and he knew Jonson could be knotty and heavy on the page, but when the lines were known (he assured them) and everyone knew what it was that they were actually saying (he didn't put it this crudely) the words would leap off the page.

He was talking to some of the best actors in the country: three of them had won Best Actor awards. They had tackled some of the biggest and most demanding roles in the repertoire. Alex Jennings, who plays Subtle, had been Hamlet at the RSC and Simon Russell Beale, who plays Face, had been Hamlet at the National. The best-known actor in the room, Ian Richardson, had never appeared at the National Theatre before, but he had been responsible for a catchphrase entering the public's consciousness. As the machiavellian Chief Whip Francis Urquhart in the TV series *House of Cards*, he would murmur, "You might very well say that. I couldn't possibly comment." In his stage career, Richardson had been a founding member of the RSC, appearing in legendary Shakespeare productions as Coriolanus and Richard II. For those in the rehearsal room who had gone along to these productions as teenagers, or who had since read some theatre history, it was like standing alongside a member of the 1966 World Cup team.

Some of those in the rehearsal room had spent years and years in one Shakespeare production or another and had spoken millions of lines of blank verse. But even with these actors, even after a four-day workshop in which lots of user-friendly tweaks had been made and during which 700 lines had been cut (so the audience could head home by 10.30), even after all that, it still didn't seem like a good idea to sit down and read *The Alchemist* out loud.

At this moment, it was hard not to feel sympathy for those English teachers across the country who were teaching *The Alchemist* for A level (it was on the syllabus). Here was a group of highly experienced, motivated and intelligent people, and they were about to be devoting themselves for several weeks to the task of figuring out what the play was saying. What chance did anyone else have?

The cast were going to begin on page one and work their way through, line by line, to page 108. They would ask two main questions: what does it mean and how do we say it so that it makes sense? And every time they came across a problem they would apply the Zammo test. In seven weeks the play would open in front of an audience of 1,200 people in the Olivier theatre; 800 of whom had paid £10. This was a production that aimed to have a broad appeal. The last sound anyone wanted to hear was a few chuckles from academics in the audience who knew their 17th century English literature.

There were half a dozen problems on page one: "lick figs"; "out of all your sleights"; "I'll douse your silks." Each one took some untangling. If it couldn't be untangled, they always had another option. "If we can't make clear what something means," said Hytner, "cut it." Nothing was going to be allowed to be obscure. He had given the company the single reason why people were going to come and see this play. "Because it's funny," he said, "It has to be funny."

## Day 2: Tuesday

*The Alchemist* is set 400 years ago, but the background to the events, why some of the characters behave the way they do, goes back another 100 years. On Day Two, one of the younger actors, Sam Spruell, asked a simple enough question. He was playing the Anabaptist deacon Ananias, and he wanted to know about the religious situation at the time. For half an hour, the cast stopped going through the play line by line, and Hytner gave a run-down on the religious situation in the 16th and 17th centuries.

It went like this: the German priest Martin Luther nailed his 95 theses to the door of Wittenburg Church, attacking the abuses in the Church (this was in 1517). The Catholic Church was very corrupt at the time and Luther's attack led in Europe, particularly in Germany, Switzerland and the Netherlands, to the Protestant Reformation.

The English king Henry VIII wrote an attack against Luther, defending the Catholic Church, which pleased the Pope very much and earned Henry the title of Defender of the Faith (a title the Queen still holds). But things changed when Henry wanted to divorce his wife Catherine of Aragon to marry Anne Boleyn and the Pope refused to grant him a divorce. The church in England split with the church in Rome, Henry appointed himself head of the Church of England, and this country proceeded to have its own Reformation, with a monarch as the head of the church.

When Henry died, his nine-year-old son Edward became king and the work of the Protestant Reformation was carried forward by his Protector, Archbishop Cranmer. When Edward died six years later, his sister Mary, a devout Catholic, took the country back to Catholicism, executing those who disagreed with her (including Cranmer), and earning the nickname 'Bloody Mary'. Her reign lasted five years and she was succeeded by her half-sister, Elizabeth, who established a "religious settlement" in which England would be Protestant, but Catholics wouldn't be persecuted.

James became king of England in 1603, and held a conference at Hampton Court the following year to work out a new religious settlement. This went badly for the Puritans and Puritan clergy were excommunicated for non-conformity. This is why Ananias and Tribulation Wholesome are based in Holland and why they aren't allowed to preach in England. They are considered seditious figures. All this would have been immediately obvious to an audience in 1610.

If a character walked on stage today and announced that he or she was an anti-vivisectionist, for instance, an audience would have a good idea about what the character believed in, the kinds of political actions he or she might be involved in, and the people who might most strongly oppose this character. In 1610, an audience would have known exactly the same about an Anabaptist.

## Day 3: Wednesday

The cast were reading the scene (I.iii) in which Abel Drugger arrives to get advice on the layout of his shop and Subtle looks at Drugger's face and hands and starts to reel off some mumbo-jumbo about what he can tell from looking at them. Face pretends to be in awe at the good news that Subtle has to impart and asks how Subtle could possibly know all this so quickly. Subtle explains:

> By a rule, Captain,
> In metoposcopy, which I do work by:
> A certain star i'the forehead, which you see not.
> Your chestnut or your olive-coloured face
> Does never fail, and your long ear doth promise.
> I knew't, by certain spots, too, in his teeth,
> And on the nail of his mercurial finger.

These seven lines are not easy to follow, but when Alex Jennings read them, everyone in the room burst out laughing. They knew exactly who the character was and what the situation was. His voice had the silkily intimate tone – slightly condescending and controlling – of a New Age guru. The accent was Californian.

Simon Russell Beale was thinking of playing Face as a bluff retired naval captain. (There is a reference at the end to Face having gone to Yarmouth, "or some good port-town else, waiting for the wind".) Face would be the sort of cheery, dependable fellow who is a regular at the village pub, smoking a pipe, a labrador at his feet and his own tankard behind the bar. Russell Beale wanted a blazer, a stripey tie and a pipe. He wanted to be someone whom it would be impossible not to trust. That was the key. (As the con artist Mike says in *House of Games*: "Of course you gave me your trust. That's what I do for a living.") Russell Beale was thinking of basing the character on the most trustworthy person he knew: his father. Another name that was suggested was Kenneth More as Douglas Bader in *Reach For The Sky*. The audience must find Face to be as plausible as Dapper and Drugger find him. "He's a man in a blazer and tie going round shafting people," said Russell Beale, "It's really unpleasant. They're shits."

# Day 4: Thursday

Costumes not only affect the way people look, they affect the way people talk. In most productions the costume design has been decided at the beginning, but Hytner and Thompson had deliberately left the options open, and the cast were joining in the discussion. By Day Four the question as to which period the play might be set had come down to four options:

## 1. Set *The Alchemist* in 1610

Jonson wrote a play in 1610 about characters in 1610 that was watched by an audience in 1610. But that made it, in effect, a modern dress production. "You can't reproduce that," said Hytner, "That audience is 400 years' dead. To try and get Jacobean London right in every detail is an inauthentic option. It's not a particularly useful thing to do."

## 2. Set *The Alchemist* in 2006

"As you watch it," said Hytner, "You're still carrying the other period in your head. It's not that it makes me forget that it's set in a world 400 years ago. But you enjoy the tensions between the two." This approach wouldn't work if the play became a series of "sight gags". The current NT production of *The Life of Galileo* was in modern dress, but that wasn't in any way the point of the production. "It makes the people in it more alive and approachable," said Hytner, "The audience sit there knowing it's a 17th century story, and the modern dress helps deliver it to an audience. The reason I've baulked at a modern dress show up to now is that you do buy yourself a problem. Every page is peppered with references to the Jacobean world. You don't notice the clothes in *Galileo*, you notice that it's not a lot of people in costume booming away." Alex Jennings asked, "But how do you get around the Spaniard?" When Subtle sees Surly dressed as the Spaniard, he says, "He looks in that deep ruff like a head on a platter." Tim McMullan who plays Surly (who dresses up as the Spaniard), said: "I don't know if the comedy would be lost by updating it."

## 3. Set *The Alchemist* in the 1890s, 1950s, etc.

This third option was to pick another period that might illuminate the play (Victorian London, 1920s London, post-war London). That type of production had been done very successfully over the past 20 to 30 years, but Hytner felt that this approach had had its day.

### 4. Set The Alchemist in a "version of now"

This was slightly harder to define, but Hytner spoke of a "distanced" or "abstracted" version of now. This was not a question of picking a specific year, but of finding which things could be coherent and consistent within a single production. The point of the show would not be that it was in modern dress. They would avoid "all the accoutrements of modernity," said Hytner. "There won't be any digital or electronic equipment." They would try and avoid the audience asking: "Why doesn't he pick up the phone?" It would be a clear piece of story-telling if Subtle's alchemical assistant, Lungs, could wear a white lab coat, so long as it didn't say "Imperial College Laboratory" on it. But could Lungs wear a lab coat and the Spaniard look as if he had stepped out of a Velasquez portrait? The challenge was clear. "You want to have a ruff and a beard because it keeps saying so in the script," said Hytner, "And you want to have a blazer and a Californian accent."

## Day 5: Friday

As con artists Subtle and Face were drawing on two separate skills, which might loosely be called 'hypnosis' and 'impro'. The first is used to draw in the mark, to engage his attention so fully, like the snake in The Jungle Book with his mesmeric circling eyes, that the mark cannot take notice of anything else. The other skill the cons need is to be as quick-witted as impro artists, to pick up on what the other con – or the mark – throws at them and run with it. As Nicolas Cage says in Matchstick Men, "The most important thing you have to understand about this game is, ninety per cent of it is variable." Both skills require very high levels of concentration.

Before rehearsals began, Jennings and Russell Beale were discussing Derren Brown, the psychological illusionist, who has studied mind-reading and neuro-linguistics, and works through suggestion and misdirection. He has also trained as a magician. One of his most famous stunts (in October 2003) was Russian Roulette, when he had to guess, from studying the facial expressions of the person pulling the trigger, which chamber in the gun contained the bullet. It might be something as slight as a pupil in the eye dilating. It's a highly dramatic version of the *tell* in poker, the physical mannerism that gives away the strength or weakness of an opponent's hand.

Like an expert fortune teller or poker player, Subtle seems to pick up a lot of information about Drugger, even working out the day in the week that he was born: "His little finger. Look. You were born upon a Wednesday?" It requires total concentration from the con to get the mark to listen to everything he says and give back the clues that he needs. As Joe Mantegna's character, Mike, says in *House of Games*, "You can't bluff someone who's not paying attention."

In his 1960s novel, *The Grifters*, Jim Thompson describes the white heat of concentration required by his central character, the grifter Roy, as he cheats at dice.

> When his four dupes thought about him later, it would be as a 'helluva nice guy', so amiably troubled by his unwanted and unintended winnings as to make shameful any troubled thoughts of their own. When Roy thought about them later – but he would not. All his thinking was concentrated on *them*, the time of their fleecing; in keeping them constantly diverted and disarmed. And in the high intensity of that concentration, in fuelling its white-hot flames, he had nothing of them left for afterthoughts. They enjoyed their drinks; his were tasteless.

## Day 6: Monday

This *Alchemist* was moving further away from 1610 and closer to 2006. Hytner explained his reasons to Tim McMullan, who plays Surly (and the Spanish Don). "I spent the weekend going through the script, working out how much you gain and how much you lose by that. And the scam, the get-rich-quick, the elixir of life, you can be young again… it all feels so modern. So I think we might have to lose the ruff."

## Day 7: Tuesday

When Ananias enters the Blackfriars house, Subtle asks: "Who are you?" It's been a busy morning for Subtle as Dapper, Drugger, Sir Epicure and Surly have all been and gone. Alex Jennings wanted to know what Sam Spruell would be wearing. Spruell said, "Amish." (The Amish are the pacifist religious sect, best known for sheltering Harrison Ford in the thriller *Witness*.) Hytner said, "Amish is a red herring."

He recommended Spruell look up *Christian Voice* on the internet. They were the group that protested energetically against the National Theatre's production of *Jerry Springer – The Opera*. Hytner recommended Spruell take a look at the spokesman. "Stephen or Simon someone," said Hytner, "Just google it. He's all over the place." The stage managers had a computer in the rehearsal room with an internet link. The cast gathered round to watch a video clip from the *Christian Voice* website.

Stephen Green was standing in front of the Cambridge Theatre in the West End, where *Jerry Springer* was playing. He wore a dark jacket, white shirt and stripey tie; he had a boyish face, deep-set eyes and greying hair. Behind him were posters for the show proclaiming all the awards *Jerry Springer* had won: "Best Musical: Evening Standard Awards; Best Musical: Olivier Awards; Best Musical: Critics' Circle Awards. The video clip cut away from Stephen Green to other people from *Christian Voice* who were talking to members of the audience and handing out yellow leaflets. One of the protesters wore a woolly hat and an anorak. Alex Jennings said, "It could be a woolly hat and an anorak."

They went back to rehearsing the scene. Jonson had been having a go at extreme fundamentalists. "Start off as happy-clappy," Hytner said to Spruell, "All that smiliness can hide a lot of aggression." Spruell's Ananias could hand out leaflets. (One of the stage managers quickly found him a shoulder bag.) Subtle asked, "Who are you?" Ananias replied, "Please you, a servant of the exiled brethren, that deal with widows' and with orphans' goods." But as he said this, he might be wearing a woolly hat and an anorak, he might be smiling, and he might be carrying lots of angry leaflets in his bag. He would be a Puritan who didn't like what went on in the theatre: a timeless figure.

## Day 8: Wednesday

Playwrights can't help writing about the people they know and Jonson knew about actors. The con artists in *The Alchemist* were like actors (Hytner suggested) because they really came alive when they had a performance to give, when they were *on*. The rest of the time (he could imagine) many of these Jacobean actors were sour and argumentative; the rogues and vagabonds of the day.

The scenes when Subtle, Face and Dol are together and no one else is around are the off-duty scenes. The play opens, furiously, with one of them. There's another off-duty scene when Face returns from the Temple Church, where he has gone to look for Surly and, having failed to find Surly, has come across a Spanish Don, who will be along shortly. Face has told the Spanish Don about Dol Common, and he has come home to tell her to get herself ready. "I've got a really classy guy," said Russell Beale, "and she'd better smarten up."

When Face returns to the house from the Temple Church (Russell Beale thought) he would have to knock. "I would always knock to check that it was safe." Alex Jennings thought that Subtle would answer the door (Face wouldn't let himself in; Subtle might have a client there). To add to the air of caution, Jennings asked for a peep-hole or a letter box or both.

The mood inside the house is dark. "They don't get on," said Russell Beale. Dol brings in a cup of tea and lights a cigarette. "It's nice these moments," said Lesley Manville, who plays Dol, "when they're not on show." She suggested there might be some dirty plates and an empty bottle of wine from the night before. "It helps with the whole slovenly mood of it all." Jennings suggested various types of food might emerge from the kitchen during the day (toast at breakfast, sandwiches at lunch) to give a sense of the day passing.

Later that day, Ian Richardson said that during the weeks of rehearsal he often wakes in the middle of the night with an idea. He has a notepad by his bed and the other night he jotted down the word "Viagra". After the interval, Sir Epicure arrives at the house for his assignation with Dol. Richardson was pursuing the idea of Sir Epicure as a stage door Johnnie arriving at the house with a bunch of flowers and a bottle of champagne. Dol is supposed to be the sister of a lord, so this is as much about status as it is about sex. Before Dol arrives, Sir Epicure outlines what he means to do. "I will be puissant," he says, "and mighty in my talk to her." On the word *puissant*, Richardson pops a couple of "Viagra" pills into his mouth.

He wanted to know what Dol would be wearing? "A little black dress," said Manville, "So it looks scholarly and sexy. A sort of Audrey Hepburn look." There would be Audrey Hepburn glasses too. Sir Epicure attempts some old world courtesy by praising Dol's looks, saying that she has the nose of a Valois, the forehead of a Medici and the chin of a Hapsburg. Richardson had brought in three computer print-outs of paintings of a Hapsburg, a Valois and a Medici (which his wife had researched on the internet), and had pinned them up on the back wall. The Valois had a very long nose, the Medici had a large square forehead and the Hapsburg had a pronounced chin.

Sir Epicure assures Dol that she is wasting herself by living obscurely in this nook of Blackfriars. "Come forth, and taste the air of palaces," he says, and launches into a foodie's description of pheasants' eggs, cockles boiled in silver shells and shrimps swimming "in a rare butter made of dolphins' milk". Richardson had spent 15 years playing in Shakespeare at Stratford and reads every line for its metre. ("I'm sorry, I can't help it. It's those 15 years doing Shakespeare.") Sir Epicure may have been a little in awe of Dol when she first appears, and he may have paid her one or two unfortunate compliments, but when he talks about food he is in his element. "If there is one moment in the scene in which he knows what he is about to say, it is this," said Richardson, "The regularity of the beat is there."

## Day 9: Thursday

Half the cast had prepared background research, which they were going to present to the company. On Day 9, the tables were pushed into the centre of the room for the 'research sharing'. Each actor gave his or her talk, and in the discussion afterwards, the cast looked for modern connections and parallels.

### Puritanism

Ian Barritt plays the zealous pastor, Tribulation Wholesome. The young deacon, Ananias, is very scrupulous about what an Anabaptist can and cannot do; Tribulation thinks the ends may justify the means. He tells Ananias, "We must bend unto all means that may give furtherance to the holy cause." Barritt spoke about Puritanism.

He said the church had been corrupt in many ways: there was pluralism (holding many offices); simony (buying or selling of offices); absenteeism; and nepotism, with children appointed to be cardinals. Anabaptists did not believe in infant baptism. They were forerunners of 'born again' Christians. The name 'Anabaptist', like the name 'Puritan' originated as a term of abuse and is impossible to define exactly. Puritans wore sober dress and believed in strict sexual morality. There was no ritual, no mass, no crucifix (a cross with the figure of Jesus), and no adornments in church. They were strongest in London, East Anglia and Scotland. The theatres were closed in 1642 and reopened in 1660 when Charles II ascended the throne. The Restoration not only brought back the monarchy, it brought back theatre as well. Public reaction to Puritans is best caught by Shakespeare in *Twelfth Night* when Sir Toby Belch says: "Dost thou think, because thou art virtuous, there shall be no more cakes and ale?" Puritans were against theatres, so they were never going to get a fair press from playwrights.

## Puritanism now

The impact of Puritanism can be seen in the high-profile campaigns against abortion, blasphemy, gay rights, stem cell research, and the teaching of Darwinism, etc. Evangelical Protestantism lies at the heart of the current White House administration. The Evangelists were the four authors of the Gospels and the evangelical movement, which Luther in effect created, believed that by spreading the word of the Gospel, people would see the rightness of what he was saying. George Bush is a born again Methodist. Secretary of State Condoleezza Rice is the daughter of a Presbyterian minister. The last attorney general John Ashcroft is the son and grandson of Pentecostal ministers. As the president of the influential right-wing pressure group, Focus on the Family, wrote in 2003, "Without the hard work and votes of millions of Christians, there would be no Republican majority in both Houses of Congress, no Bush presidencies, few Republican governors and a small handful of state houses in Republican hands."

## The Plague

John Burgess plays Lovewit, the master of the house, who loves "a teeming wit" and forgives his butler Jeremy all the mischief he has done. Lovewit leaves town because of the threat of the plague. Burgess spoke about the plague.

He said the plague had been endemic in Britain since the Black Death. There were periodic flare-ups in summer and autumn with the rise of temperature. In 1610 probably more people were killed by criminal activity. It was common for the rich to leave town and there was a story of a servant, William Lilley, whose master had left him in charge of his house, who went bowling in Lincoln's Inn Fields, learnt the bass viol and attended sermons at Westminster Abbey.

When you had the plague you suffered from headaches and delirium, before sinking into a coma. A blister at the site of the flea's bite became a gangrenous blackish carbuncle. The subcutaneous spots changed colour from orange to black. Current remedies were very haphazard. There was very little fresh water. Herbal remedies were used. But women who used them were sometimes accused of being witches. Special ingredients for cures included powder called 'corn' from the mythical unicorn, spiders' webs, swallows' nests and the skulls of executed criminals.

## The Plague now

The most widely feared outbreak of plague today is avian influenza or bird flu. There was no doubt that if an outbreak of flu hit London, the rich would follow Lovewit's example, get in their 4x4s and head down the motorway to their country houses, and their London homes would be left in the care of the Filipino staff.

During the period of rehearsals information published on the Department of Health website stated that 239 people had caught the infection as a result of close contact with infected birds and 139 of those had subsequently died. "There is no firm evidence that H5N1 has acquired the ability to pass easily from person to person. However, concern remains that the virus might develop this ability, or that it might mix with human flu viruses to create a new virus. It is this ability of avian influenza to change and to mix, that has given rise to the fear of a new human flu pandemic." (15 August 2006)

## Alchemy

Jason Cheater plays one of the neighbours who keep a suspicious eye on the house and tell Lovewit, when he returns, what they think has been happening. Cheater spoke about alchemy.

He said it was estimated that over 100,000 books have been written on alchemy, possibly more than on any other subject in history. Alchemy has been known as the Royal Art, the Divine Art and the Art of Transformation. Once it became known that alchemy supposedly had the power to make the practitioner immensely wealthy, the art began to attract frauds. They were known as "puffers", a reference to the bellows used to maintain the laboratory fire.

Alchemists saw themselves as furthering a natural process, the refining of less exalted matter, like base metal, in accordance with the real but hidden order of the universe. Some alchemists viewed the metaphysical aspects of their work as the true foundation of alchemy. The transmutation of base metal into gold symbolised the evolution from an imperfect, diseased and corruptible state to one of enlightenment. Alchemical books were profusely illustrated. The imagery frequently shows the king and queen engaging in sexual intercourse.

Most alchemists adhered to the basic sequence of nigredo to albedo to rubedo. The initial stage, nigredo, or the blackening stage, deals with raw confused mass. The second stage, albedo, deals with cleansing or whitening the matter. The final stage of the work, ribedo, or the reddening, is the climax when the Philosopher's Stone, or the Elixir of Life, is produced. A central idea was that everything in the world is unified. Everything is related to everything else.

### Alchemy now

The kind of holistic world view that alchemists expressed feels very modern: close to the outlook of theoretical physicists or environmentalists, such as James Lovelock in *Gaia*. During rehearsals, the *New York Times* reported on a conference about alchemy and quoted a history professor at Columbia saying alchemy was the "matter theory of its day" and was "incredibly multi-layered and therefore a powerful way of viewing nature".

### Quarrelling

Elisabeth Dermot Walsh plays Dame Pliant, the 19-year-old widow, who is referred to as soft, buxom and rich, and also as good, dull and innocent. Dame Pliant has very few lines and Hytner wondered whether this was because the part was originally played by a boy, who turned out to be a really bad actor and more and more of his lines were cut. Dermot Walsh was determined to introduce a range of squeaks and squeals to fill out her role.

Tristan Beint plays her brother Kastril, the country bumpkin who has come up to London to be one of the roaring boys. (A kestrel is a small, angry falcon.) He has inherited £3,000 a year (millions today) and has come to the city to acquire some style. He has heard "some speech of the boys and seen 'em take tobacco...and would fain be one of 'em".

Dermot Walsh said that in the Jacobean period people were short-tempered; disagreements blew up quickly and everyone was encouraged to carry a weapon. There was much less domestic violence and much more public brawling in the street. If you insulted someone it was taken very seriously, even if you were drunk or it was a mistake. Ben Jonson had killed a fellow actor. It's impossible to find out why – maybe the other actor upstaged him, or coughed during his lines.

Beint said that Shakespeare outlines the art of the quarrel in *As You Like It* when Touchstone explains about the *retort courteous*, which is the polite denial, the *quip modest*, which is a witty reply, the *reply churlish*, which is a curt reply, the *reproof valiant*, which is the honourable response, running through to the *counter check quarrelsome*, *lie circumstantial* and the *lie direct*, which is flat denial with aggression.

Dermot Walsh said it was possible to be very rude to someone by not speaking to them. Again, there were degrees. The *cut direct* is when you look someone straight in the face and don't acknowledge them. The *cut indirect* is when you glance the other way and pretend not to see them. The *cut sublime* is when you don't see them because you are busy admiring something very beautiful in the distance. The *cut infernal* is when you stop and do up your shoe laces, so that you don't see the other person as he walks past.

## Quarrelling now

"Yo' Momma's so ugly...when she walks into a bank, they turn the cameras off."

"Yo' Momma's so poor I saw her kicking a can down the street. I asked her what she was doin' and she said, 'Moving'."

"Yo' Momma's so fat... God created her and on the seventh day he rested."

These three quotes are taken from the Wikipedia entry for "the dozens", an oral tradition in which African-American men go head-to-head in a contest of trash-talk; in its most basic form, it is a succession of insults about the other person's mother. There are two important ways in which "the dozens", this form of wise-cracking abuse, is similar to quarrelling in Kastril's time. One is that it is a battle of wits. (No one is going to wait for your reply.) The other is that it was a way of sublimating or controlling violence. The cast had been puzzling over Kastril's strange desire to come to London and learn how to quarrel (it seemed faintly implausible) until the discussion turned to its similarity with "the dozens". Kastril wants to sharpen his wits. He wants to be hip.

## Spain, or the rise of Johnnie Foreigner

Tim McMullan plays Pertinax Surly, the gamester and card player, who is sharp enough to see what's happening. ("I would not willingly be gulled.") He returns to the house disguised as the Spanish Don. As one of the characters says in the movie *Confidence*: "In any con, sooner or later somebody is going to start asking the right questions." McMullan spoke about Spain, or the rise of Johnnie Foreigner.

He said that in those days monarchs were like chief executives of multi-national companies, busily involved in takeovers and mergers which they achieved through invasion or marriage. Spain was part of an enormous empire under Charles V, which included Austria, Germany, Spain, North Africa and parts of the Americas. The Spanish had come over to England for the wedding of Philip II to Queen Mary (1555) and found the weather wet and rainy and the English pink and quarrelsome. Mary was getting on, she was 38, and Philip was 11 years younger. When Mary came to the throne she was popular, but when she started burning people and married a Spaniard, she became unpopular. The Spanish were involved in a bitter war with the Dutch. Whole towns were starved to death. Part of the plan was to remove Elizabeth I because she wasn't the true heir. Elizabeth was not only a bastard but a heretic.

England was very threatened by Catholic Spain. To be a Catholic became synonymous with being a traitor, and anyone who was Spanish was mistrusted. Spanish galleons were large ocean-going vessels and very slow; English ships were small and nippy and could fire rapidly. During the Armada, when the Spanish ships failed to meet up with troops in the Netherlands, the English set some of their own knackered ships on fire and, with the prevailing winds, sent them into the middle of the Armada. After the defeat of the Armada, the Spaniards became figures of fun.

## Spain now

The sight of the Spanish Don would have had the same frisson as the sight of a German officer in London in the early 1960s. If Basil Fawlty had been in charge of a tavern in 1610 and had Spanish guests he would have been running around saying, "Don't mention the Armada!"

The Spanish were the big European power of the period, as the British were in the 20th century. For Ananias and Tribulation, the Spanish had been a far more recent and bitter enemy.

## Tobacco

Amit Shah was playing Abel Drugger as a first generation Indian shopkeeper. Drugger would have had no resources to fall back on, his shop *has* to succeed. Shah spoke about tobacco.

He said tobacco was first brought to England in the second half of the 16th century. Sir Francis Drake had come across tobacco in the Americas and introduced it to Sir Walter Raleigh who set off for the Americas. By 1586 smoking had taken root in English society. It was the trendy new drug. Initially, its pleasure was confined to the wealthy classes, but its use soon spread. In 1600 Pope Clement VIII issued a ban on smoking in holy places. That same year Sir Walter Raleigh persuaded Queen Elizabeth to try some. James I strongly disapproved of tobacco, but instead of banning it, he raised the duty on importing tobacco to unprecedented levels. Tobacco became very expensive for the consumer. By the mid-17th century, there were 7,000 shops in London.

### Tobacco now

The modern equivalent to tobacco would be some fashionable new drug.

## Life of Ben Jonson

Alex Jennings, who plays Subtle, occasionally writes entries on distinguished actors for the *Dictionary of National Biography*. His research for his talk on Jonson drew on the DNB's own entry on Jonson.

Ben Jonson was of Scottish descent and had a keen interest in Scotland. The Johnstones – there were 13 ways of spelling the name, but always with a 't' – were brigands and warlords. At Westminster the pupils regularly performed a Latin play and Jonson developed a lifelong affection for plays by Plautus and Terence. Jonson was unable to go to university and went to work for his step-father as a bricklayer. He was taunted throughout his life about this.

John Aubrey records that Jonson "was never a good actor, but an excellent instructor". In his play *The Staple of News* (1626) Jonson has the character Gossip Mirth speak of the author in a sweaty agitation giving last-minute instructions to the actors. The actor Gabriel Spencer, whom Jonson killed in a duel, had challenged Jonson to the duel, had fought with a sword that was 10 inches longer than Jonson's, and had wounded Jonson first. Jonson had been away from home when his son Benjamin died, but he had a vision of the boy appearing before him as an adult with the mark of a bloody cross on his forehead.

When Queen Elizabeth died, Jonson made no attempt to mourn her death in writing, but composed speeches for three pageants to welcome James I's royal entry to London. He went to prison again in 1605 when *Eastward Ho!* was performed because the play refers to the lavish distribution of knighthoods (for which James I was responsible) and because of the actors' mimicry of Scottish accents. The next year, Jonson wrote *Volpone* in five weeks.

Jonson spent money as fast as it came in. In later years he weighed 20 stone. He had been a slender man but developed a mountainous belly and a rocky face. When he walked to Edinburgh he stayed with the poet William Drummond, who left a record of Jonson's tart remarks on Donne and Shakespeare. Jonson became the first unofficial poet laureate.

### Ben Jonson now

Jennings thought that Jonson was bit of a geezer, a boozer, a ducker-and-diver, and hard. He was a bastard. "But I bet he was fun to be with," said Hytner, "He sounds like John Osborne."

### London

Andrew McDonald plays one of the neighbours. He spoke about London.

London had become the legal, financial, political and social centre of the country. Many of the streets were narrow, crowded with wagons and animals, noisy with traders' cries, and darkened by overhanging buildings. Mid-street gutters and open drains made it filthy underfoot. In these areas disease was rife. The open drains of Fleetditch and Moorditch were often clogged and stinking, causing typhoid. Marshy areas, such as the South Bank (where the National Theatre now is) produced malaria.

The Fleet river, which flows from Hampstead and Highgate into the Thames at Blackfriars, became an open sewer running red with the blood of animals slaughtered at Smithfield market. A hundred years later, according to the satirist Jonathan Swift, it was still full of "sweepings from butchers' stalls, dung, guts and blood, drowned puppies, stinking sprats, all drenched in mud, dead cats and turnip tops, which came tumbling down the flood". The first pumped water supply was installed in 1581, and pumped supplies gradually replaced inefficient gravity conduits.

The rapid rise in population was largely caused by immigration from the rest of the country where the birth rate was high. About 7,000 people a year migrated to London. Many of these were rootless poor, lured by the hope of London wages, which were 50% higher than those in the provinces.

## London now

It was horrible then. Complaints about congestion charges and cyclists on pavements seem trivial in comparison.

## Day 10: Friday

The fairies were going to be like the elves in *The Lord of the Rings*. Jonson's dialogue for the fairies goes "ti, ti, ti, ti, to, ta" and "ti, ti, do, ti, ti do, ti da". In rehearsals they were discussing how to do the high-pitched voices, when Jennings suggested using helium. If they used canisters, one of the stage managers pointed out, the Health and Safety regulations wouldn't allow them to inhale directly from the canisters. They could have the helium in balloons, but how many balloons would they need? They would have to inhale a lungful of helium after they delivered each line. Lesley Manville as Dol would be at the top of the stairs, playing the Irish harp and singing. Bryan Dick as Dapper would be standing on a chair, blind-folded and wearing a petticoat. Jennings and Russell Beale would be pinching Dapper, speaking to him as Subtle and Face, and doing the *ti-ti-to-das* of the fairies, which they would also translate for Dapper. Were they going to add helium balloons to all this? Russell Beale said, "I think the real problem is an artistic one. Why would they be doing it?" Hytner said, "If I thought there wasn't enough funny stuff going on..." Jennings said, "You'd be bringing on the helium." Hytner said, "I'd be bringing on the helium."

## Day 11: Monday

The first neighbour will be a taxi controller; the second neighbour will be a baker; the third will be a blacksmith; the fourth a maid; the fifth neighbour will be a greengrocer; the sixth works in John Lewis; and a seventh neighbour has been added, who works as a bank clerk.

## Day 12: Tuesday

One of the actors told a story in rehearsals about how he was conned out of a couple of thousand dollars. The way it happened was this: he had been appearing in a play in New York and was walking back to his hotel after an evening performance when he was approached by a man in a state of anxiety. The man was looking for his hotel. He had already paid for his room at the Port Authority, but he couldn't find the hotel. The actor helped him search the nearby streets for where it was (they were very close) but they couldn't find it. The actor telephoned the New York version of directory enquiries. No luck. The man had a wad of money on him, which he kept producing (to the alarm of the actor) to prove that he didn't need money.

A woman and child walked past and the actor called after them and asked for help. They turned and came back. The actor explained that the man was looking for his hotel. The woman said the hotel didn't exist anymore. The man was very distressed: what was he going to do? (This was a white town, he said, he was a black guy, he didn't have a chance...)

The actor suggested the man stay at the YMCA. The woman offered to drive him there. The man was very worried that he would have his money stolen. He had a lot of money on him. The actor offered to put the man's money in his own safe deposit at his hotel. So they went back to the actor's hotel, the actor showed them the safe deposit and how it worked and the man said he would feel a lot better about his money if the actor's money was with his in the safe deposit box. The man was in considerable distress and the actor agreed.

So this is what they did: the actor's money and the man's money went in the safe deposit box (he would collect it tomorrow) and the woman drove the man to the YMCA. After a while, when the actor was alone in his hotel room, he thought he would prefer to separate his money from the other man's money. He went to the safe deposit box, took out the money, and he found there was nothing in the bag but torn-up newspaper. He had been the victim of a switch.

He could remember the moment. The woman never talked to the other man. She only talked to the actor. But when the actor was in the process of taking the man's money, and putting the man's money and his own in the bag, he remembered that the woman had said he should tuck his shirt in, because he looked untidy. He remembered looking down at his shirt and thinking, it *is* tucked in.

## Day 13: Wednesday

The arrival of the police officers in the last act would be a Keystone Cops moment. There are loud knocks on the door and Sir Epicure shouts, "Cheaters, bawds, conjurers!" Outside, the officers threaten to break down the door. From inside the house, Lovewit asks if they have a warrant. One of the officers says, "Warrant enough." Surly shouts, "Down with the door!" Kastril shouts, "Ding it open!" Ananias calls the house's occupants "Scorpions and caterpillars".

Lovewit opens the door and the officers and neighbours tumble indoors and onto the floor. General commotion ensues. Jonson provides precise directions within the dialogue as to how he would like the scene to be played. They must be talking at the same time as the police officer says, "One after another gentlemen, I charge you."

Lovewit allows them to explore his house ("The doors are open") and they push on through to search the rooms. For the purposes of rehearsals, each of the doors has been marked with a large capital letter: Door E is where Dame Pliant gets married. Door D is the storage area where all the pewter is kept. Door G is the laboratory. Door F is the kitchen. The main set isn't in the rehearsal room, but the doors, or versions of them, are in place. Ten of them. It looks like the backstage act in *Noises Off*.

## Day 14: Thursday

The stage directions at the very start of the play say: *Enter Face in a Captain's uniform with his sword drawn and Subtle with a vial, quarrelling, and Dol Common*. Traditionally, the opening of the play goes at breakneck speed. Face says, "Believe't, I will." Subtle says, "Thy worst. I fart at thee." Dol says, "Ha' you your wits. Why, gentlemen!"

Jennings, Russell Beale and Manville were not going to be arguing at breakneck speed. They would be eating breakfast and they would be fuming. There would be plates with bacon and eggs on them, there would be knives and forks and mugs, and a teapot, a toast rack, and sauce bottles. Russell Beale wouldn't have a sword, he would have a kitchen knife. Jennings wouldn't have a vial, he would have a bottle of bleach. No one would speak. The row would be simmering away, until – in the actors' own time, when they felt like it – the argument could start up again. When Subtle says he farts at Face, he would fart first, and then say the line by way of explanation. The sound department had been asked to supply either a remote controlled fart machine to be placed in a drawer in the table or the sound effect of a fart.

## Day 15: Friday

When Sir Epicure brings Surly along to the house to witness Subtle's genius as an alchemist, Surly's scepticism prompts Subtle into a detailed explanation about the principles of alchemy and how one species can emerge out of another. Bees, hornets, beetles and wasps emerge out of the dung of creatures. In the same way, gold will one day emerge from the combination of metals that he is mixing.

Jennings asks for chemicals to play with when he explains the philosophy of alchemy. He wants brightly coloured liquids. One of the test tubes needs to have a silver liquid to look like mercury. Another looks like sulphur. The liquids would need to fizz.

## Day 16: Monday

When Drugger arrives with some tobacco as a gift for Face and Subtle it will be in a clear plastic bag and will look like marijuana. Subtle will have a lighter and some king size Rizlas in the table drawer. "'Tis good tobacco, this!" says Subtle, after he has rolled himself a joint, "What is't an ounce?"

## Day 17: Tuesday

There's a scene in the con movie *Heist* when Gene Hackman is buying a coffee (just before doing a job) and the coffee cart man says, "Hey buddy, you forgot your change." Hackman collects his change and says to his partner, "Makes the world go round." His partner asks, "What's that?" Hackman says, "Gold." His partner says, "Some people say love." Hackman replies, "They're right too. It is love. Love of gold."

He might have been talking about Face. When Face returns from the Temple Church he gets out his pocketbook and works out how much money he has made that day. He has had a run of luck. He's got £10 from Sir Epicure, £3 from the clerk, a sovereign from Drugger, 100 marks off the Anabaptists (a mark is more than £2) and he's still expecting money from the widow and the Spanish Don. But Face counts the pennies as well as the pounds.

As they prepare Dapper to meet the Queen of the Fairies they still fleece him for everything he has got. He hands over 120 shillings for the Queen of the Fairies' servants, an old Harry's sovereign, three James shillings, an Elizabeth groat and 20 nobles. As soon as the fairies start pinching Dapper he hands over another sovereign that he has kept in a piece of paper, and then he hands over his gold bracelet (half a crown). They do not leave him empty-handed. Subtle presents him with a dead mouse and some gingerbread, which the Queen of the Fairies has sent. Subtle would find the mouse in a mousetrap under the stairs and the gingerbread would be a ginger biscuit. After that, they lock him in the loo.

## Day 18: Wednesday

When Surly appears as the Spaniard he will be wearing high fashion Versace-style trousers, possibly with stuffing in the crotch area. He may have a false beard. The references to his ruff have been cut from the script.

## Day 19: Thursday

The stage management requested the sound department to provide an explosion sound effect for the next day.

## Day 20: Friday

There were rehearsing the moment that Face, Subtle and Dol blow off Sir Epicure. Dol's ravings have led her to try and unzip Sir Epicure's trousers and embrace him. Face discovers that Sir Epicure had mentioned Moses and Face tells Sir Epicure to "stop her mouth". (Give her a kiss.) At the moment that Sir Epicure leans over the table to kiss the prostrate Dol, Subtle's booming voice can be heard, "What's to do there?"

As if panicking, Dol grabs hold of Sir Epicure, and Subtle enters to discover them *in flagrante delicto*. He rises to the heights of a Shakespearean tragedian.

How! What sight is here?
Close deeds of darkness, and that shun the light.

When Subtle takes in the full horror of the situation, he says, in tones that would not disgrace a mournful King Lear,

O, I have lived too long.

He tells Sir Epicure that there has been no progress in the alchemical experiment for the last half hour and now he sees the reason. He demands to know:

Where is the instrument of wickedness,
My lewd false drudge?

The terrified Sir Epicure hastens to defend Face, saying that it was not Face's fault that he saw Dol by chance. As Subtle explains how long this will retard his work, there is a great crack and explosion and the sound of cries from Face.

(The stage management played the sound effect in the rehearsals. Hytner said, "The door is going to be blown off its hinges and there will be a great cloud of smoke.")

Face appears in the doorway and says,

O sir, we are defeated! All the works
Are thrown *in fumo*, every glass is burst!

Subtle falls in a swoon. There is a knock on the door. (Russell Beale does the knock and then looks to see who is there.) It is Dol's brother, he says (whom Sir Epicure believes is a lord). The brother's coach is at the door. The brother looks furious.

Sir Epicure realises that it is all his fault.

O my voluptuous mind! I am justly punished.

It looks as if Subtle is about to expire. The angry brother is at the door. The only thing that Sir Epicure can do is hurry away. Face steers him out of the house by the back entrance. "This way, for fear the lord should meet you." Sir Epicure exits.

There is silence. The two con artists wait. Then very quietly, Subtle asks:

Face?
Ay.
Is he gone?
Yes.

And Subtle gets up from the ground and the two of them get on with the next job. It's like the end of *The Sting*.

It was also the end of the fourth week of rehearsals. The main outlines of the production were in place. They had another three weeks to go. Over the first four weeks, the gap between 1610 and 2006 had closed very significantly. The concern had always been how best to tell Jonson's story to an audience today. The cast would be performing this comedy night after night in front of 1,200 people. They had to take the audience with them. It had to be funny.

The journey in the rehearsal room had started, very firmly, in 1610, with the cast working out exactly what each line meant and why it was there. One of the aids to understanding the world in which the play had been written, and in which the action was set, was some background notes that I had compiled. The notes drew on a wide variety of books (most of them easily obtainable) and the sources were given in the text, as well as at the end. What follows, then, is the same A–Z guide that was handed out to the *Alchemist* cast on day one of rehearsals.

RB
*June – August 2006*
*National Theatre, London SE1*

# 8. The A–Z guide

> You know how you fantasise about living at different times? I would choose the first decade of the seventeenth century – as just so alive and so full... As I wrote the book I completely fell in love with the time.
>
> Adam Nicolson, author of *Power and Glory*,
> an account of the creation of the King James Bible

## ACTING
There was no acting to compare with modern stage realism (very little introspection, for instance). The interaction between actor and spectator was "open and non-illusionistic". (Styan)

## ACTORS
Like Hollywood in the 1920s, theatre in London in the late 16th century grew very quickly from a small-scale business into a major industry. Older professional actors had been strolling players, moving from town to town, and getting by on a handful of scripts. Actors who found regular work in London had far, far more lines to learn. London playhouses presented a different show every afternoon and the demand for new work was voracious. The theatre manager Philip Henslowe presented 15 shows in a month. (Henslowe was the hapless Geoffrey Rush character in *Shakespeare in Love*; the one who never changed his clothes, despite being in an Oscar-winning costume drama.) The rapid turnaround in plays was only possible in an age that placed a high value on memory skills. Work was hard, pay was low. A jobbing actor in 1610 would have received the same as a bricklayer's apprentice (and that was Ben Jonson's first job).

## 'ALCHEMIST, THE'
A comedy which "places a premium on amoral intelligence". (Barton)

## ALCHEMY
The pursuit of the Philosopher's Stone, also called the red stone, which would turn base metal into gold. Alchemy has been studied since ancient times in India, China and Egypt. The word comes from 'Al-Kemia' which means 'the Black Land', or Egypt, a name derived

from the black soil of the Nile. Alchemy disappeared after the fall of Rome and reappeared in 12th century Europe, when it was translated from the Arabic into Latin. Alchemy is the forerunner of chemistry. The well-established connection between alchemy and science persisted through the 17th century; one of the giants of modern science, Isaac Newton, made many secret alchemical investigations. Alchemy was also a spiritual quest. Transmutation could not be achieved unless the adept (one skilled in the practice) had purged himself of all vices, particularly the vice of covetousness. The alchemist "could not make gold until he had ceased to want to do so". (Thomas) As Surly says, "he who has the stone must be a pious, holy and religious man". Sir Epicure's way round this conundrum is to find a man who is religious and then buy the stone from him. This contradiction lies at the heart of Jonson's attack on alchemy. In a two-line poem he teases alchemists for their lack of material success.

If all you boast of your great art be true;
Sure, willing poverty lives most in you.

A central idea in alchemy is that all things are living and since they are living they are able to change from one shape to another. Not only are they living, but they are waiting to be released into the next stage. Just as the egg will hatch and turn into the chicken, lead is waiting to turn into gold. The main philosophical underpinning comes from Aristotle. It is the theory that there is only one ultimate 'matter' and that it can take an infinite number of 'forms'. A good example of the relationship between matter and form is iron and rust, where something has changed and something persists. "That which persists was called matter, that which changes was called form." (Taylor) To turn copper into gold required first removing the copper. This could be done by heating it with sulphur, so that it became a black mass (copper sulphide). The next step is harder: turning the black mass into gold. There were 12 stages in alchemy running from 'calcination' and 'dissolution' through to 'multiplication' and 'projection'. Alchemists used arcane language to protect their craft ("hiding a secret openly") and this elaborate jargon allowed fraudsters to flourish. In the late 14th century, Chaucer attacks fake alchemists in *The Canon's Yeoman's Tale*. Jonson's friend, the poet John Donne, was fascinated by the metaphorical aspects of alchemy. In the 20th century, the leading writer on the imaginative and symbolic aspects of alchemy was the psychologist Carl Jung. "If alchemy is ever possible," the critic Alvin

Kernan writes, "then its true powers are the wit and quickness of such characters as Face and Subtle, who always manage to turn a dollar somehow... turning the rough opportunities of life into pure gold."

## ALEMBIC

A vessel used in the distilling apparatus for holding the distilled material. The French writer Denis Diderot described the many Dutch smokers and drinkers he came across in his travels as "living alembics, distilling, in effect, themselves".

## ALMANAC

A guide to daily life that gave astrological advice on which days to pursue which activities; usually closely allied to the phases of the moon. Eg: sow crops when the moon waxes, harvest crops when the moon wanes.

## AMSTERDAM

Tribulation and Ananias are from Amsterdam. In the 17th century the port of Amsterdam became the hub of Dutch expansion, well-known for its militant clergy and for its numerous prostitutes soliciting round the docks. By 1590 Amsterdam had 180 breweries. (Schama)

## ANABAPTISTS

The two Puritans in *The Alchemist*, the pastor Tribulation Wholesome and the deacon Ananias, are members of the Anabaptist sect, the Brethren of Amsterdam. The name Anabaptist came from their belief in adult baptism (they wouldn't baptise a baby: a baby wouldn't know what it believed in). Tribulation and Ananias would know what they believed in: the idea of the separation of church and state; the Bible as the source of truth; the primacy of the individual conscience; community of goods (no private property); and the church as a voluntary association of believers. In short, they were communists who believed in God.

## ANIMALS

Dogs, baboons, puffins, stags, otters, bats, locusts, grasshoppers, puffins, bees, hornets, wasps: for a play set in the city of London, *The Alchemist* mentions a great many animals and insects. It is part of Jonson's satiric vision that humans are likened to other creatures. In *Volpone* the characters' names indicate the attributes they possess: Volpone, the magnifico, is the fox; Mosca, the parasite, is the fly;

Voltore, the lawyer, is the vulture; Corbaccio, the old gentleman, is the crow; and Corvino, the spruce merchant, is the raven.

## ANNE OF DENMARK
When she married James I in 1589 Anne had been a beauty, but now she was considered giddy and stupid. Her principal interests were "extravagant clothes and new jewels". (Kenyon)

## ARISTOPHANES
Two classical playwrights stand out as obvious inspirations for Ben Jonson. One is Plautus (see below); the other is Aristophanes. Like Jonson, the work of the Athenian playwright reflected the society in which he lived: coarse, earthy and packed with rogues and low-lifes. In most of Aristophanes' plays, "a character or small group of characters conceives an improbable and extravagant idea". Likewise, both *Volpone* and *The Alchemist* centre upon "a fantastic and seemingly untenable idea". (Barton)

## ASTROLOGY
Most people in Jacobean England believed in astrology. If parents could afford it, they would have a child's horoscope cast at birth. Astrology fitted in, seamlessly enough, with the way people viewed the world. In *King Lear* (1605), Shakespeare has Gloucester note how "these late eclipses in the sun and moon portend no good to us". Astronomy is the study of the movements of the heavenly bodies; astrology is the study of the connections between those movements and human events. But the terms 'mathematician', 'conjuror', 'astronomer' and 'astrologer' were often blurred. There were four main areas of astrology: general predictions, nativities, elections, horary questions. General predictions referred to the future movement of the heavens and how that would affect the harvest, wars, etc. Nativities were maps of the sky made on the date of someone's birth. Elections compared the information from the nativities with the current state of the heavens and predicted what course of action might be advantageous. Horary questions looked at the state of the heavens at the time the question was asked. As the experimental techniques of modern science developed during the 17th century, astrology lost its prestige. In John Wilson's play *The Cheats* (1662), the astrologer Mopus laments the decline of his trade. By the end of 17th century, when Congreve writes *Love for Love* (1695), the astrologer, named Foresight, has become the butt of jokes. (Thomas)

## BAD LANGUAGE

In May 1606 an Act of Parliament was passed to restrain the Abuses of Players. The aim was to curb profanity in the theatre and the Act carried a fine of £10 which, coincidentally, equalled the most a playwright was likely to earn from a play. The Act proved an effective instrument of self-censorship (partly because it was so vague). The historian Michael Wood shows how Shakespeare's plays were affected by comparing the Quarto version of *Othello*, thought to be pre-1606 with the revised Folio text which was published in 1623. "The first version contains more than fifty oaths and profanities," Wood writes, "The Folio text has none."

## 'BARTHOLOMEW FAIR'

The fair was job centre, market, amusement arcade, sports ground, music hall, cafe and casino. The two largest fairs were Stourbridge, near Cambridge, and St Bartholomew's, at Smithfield, London. (Salgãdo) It was at the Stourbridge Fair that the young Isaac Newton bought a book on alchemy. Bartholomew Fair was the only big city fair in England. Ben Jonson's play *Bartholomew Fair* (1614) has a cast of more than 40 speaking parts. The rude vitality of the fair, a world of rope-dancers, puppets and roast pork, is contrasted with the narrow vision of the hair-splitting Puritan, Rabbi Zeal-of-the-Land Busy, who is on the lookout for signs of idolatry.

## BIBLE, THE

One of the great achievements of the Jacobean era was the King James Authorised Version of The Bible, published in 1611, the year after *The Alchemist* was first performed. This new version, planned since 1604, has been described as the greatest work of art to have been designed by a committee. (Some say this accolade belongs to the TV series *Friends*.) The Roman Catholic Church had opposed translating the Bible from Latin, and the widespread publication of Bibles into a language that ordinary people could understand had been a major feature of the Reformation, allowing people to read the Bible in their own homes, and encouraging the spread of Puritanism, with its emphasis on private piety and the individual conscience. Nevertheless, the religiosity of the age can be overstated. The 17th century pamphleteer John Gaule argued that more people consulted almanacs as a guide to their daily actions than the Bible.

## BINGE DRINKING

The reason 16th century Englishmen were considered "great drunkards" (in the eyes of a young Venetian merchant) was the custom of "pledging", which was when one person drained the glass by drinking the health of the other; this gesture of goodwill could be repeated many times in the course of an evening.

## 'BLACKADDER'

In the fourth episode of *Blackadder the Second*, Lord Percy tells Blackadder that he has decided to discover the secret of alchemy.

> BLACKADDER: I see. And the fact that this secret has eluded the most intelligent people since the dawn of time doesn't dampen your spirits?

> PERCY: Oh, no. I like a challenge.

Later Percy emerges in the hallway, blasted and bruised: he has failed to create a lump of gold; he has succeeded in creating a lump of green. (Curtis, Elton, et al)

## BLACK ARTS

There was a profitable line of sensational journalism in writing "cony-catching" pamphlets that explained the black arts of the London underworld. The leading exponent of this genre, Robert Greene, also the author of the folklore play *Friar Bacon and Friar Bungay*, is best-remembered as the man who dismissed Shakespeare as an "upstart crow".

## BLACKFRIARS ('THE FRIARS')

The area in which Jonson lived, in which *The Alchemist* is set, and in which the play was first performed. On the north bank of the Thames, Blackfriars had been a monastery for Dominican friars since the 13th century and (for this reason) fell outside the jurisdiction of the city. In the 1600s it had become a fashionable area, the Notting Hill of its day. The streets had been laid with stones; the centre of city life, St Paul's, was close by; and it wasn't necessary to cross the river to see a show. Also, situated to the west of the city, it was upwind of the prevailing south-westerly breeze (sparing residents the worst of the smells). In 1607, Ben Jonson became a home-owner in St Anne's, Blackfriars. In 1613, Shakespeare signed the deeds to buy the gatehouse to Blackfriars, next to the theatre.

## BLACKFRIARS THEATRE

After the Dissolution of the Monasteries, the Master of the Revels, Sir Thomas Carwarden, used the convent at Blackfriars as a storage space for props from the court revels. The actor-manager James Burbage bought the theatre in Blackfriars in 1596, but wealthy residents successfully petitioned Parliament to close it on the grounds that it would "grow to be a very great annoyance". In 1608, the Blackfriars was acquired by the leading theatre company of the day, the King's Men. There were seven lessors, one of whom was Shakespeare, each paying a seventh of the rent. The Blackfriars was as different to the Globe as the National's Cottesloe is to the Olivier. The Blackfriars was smaller and more expensive, charging sixpence for admission and an extra shilling for a seat (on a bench) in the pit. If you wanted to sit on-stage, you paid even more. Its location, ticket price and repertoire made the Blackfriars a favourite with courtiers and lawyers. A thousand law students were resident during term time, many of whom had money to spend. "There was no comparison between the Globe on a cold damp afternoon," writes the Shakespeare scholar Frank Kermode, "and the shelter and comparative warmth of the indoor theatre, bright with candlelight and offering the subtler music of lutes rather than the drums and trumpets of the Globe. The rich, in their boxes or on the stage, were now closest to the action..."

## BOND, EDWARD

British playwright who wrote *Bingo* (1973) in which Shakespeare and Jonson meet shortly before Shakespeare's death. Jonson tells Shakespeare: "Shall I tell you something about me? I hate. Yes – isn't that interesting! I keep it well hidden but it's true: I hate. A short hard word. Begins with a hiss and ends with a spit: hate."

## BREAKFAST

Often beer and bread. Beer was a basic ingredient in the diet, for children too. Milk was not considered a drink for adults.

## BROTHELS

There was a close link between theatres and brothels. Most theatre-managers, like Philip Henslowe and his son-in-law Edward Alleyn, owned "stews". This state of affairs upset the Oxford-educated Stephen Gosson, who had gone from writing plays to writing pamphlets attacking theatres that put plays on (an easy journey to make). He accused playhouses of being no more than ante-rooms to brothels. "Trugging houses" or "pick-hatches" were usually situated in the suburbs (especially Southwark) because they were outside the city limits and beyond the city's jurisdiction. Shakespeare alludes to this in *Julius Caesar* when Portia asks her husband Brutus if she is truly his wife or "Dwell I but in the suburbs of your good pleasure? If it be no more, Portia is Brutus' harlot, not his wife."

## CANDLES

There were two main types of lighting in Jacobean England: daylight and candlelight. The latter was only a modest step up from darkness. The light from a single electric bulb is 100 times stronger than the light from a candle.

## CHARING CROSS

As a child, Jonson lived in the village of Charing, just east of the city of Westminster, and a mile from the city of London. His home was a workman's cottage in Hartshorn Lane, which ran from the Strand down to the Thames. A short distance from his home was "The Bermudas", a warren of alleyways, rife with prostitution and crime.

## CHEMICAL WEDDING, THE

Many alchemists believed the Philosopher's Stone was compounded of pure sulphur and mercury. That combination represents the union of the sun (Sol) and the moon (Luna), which is the union of male and female, of Hermes and Aphrodite. This produces the figure of the hermaphrodite, the embodiment of masculine and feminine characteristics.

## CHILDREN'S COMPANIES

Those who wrote for children's companies enjoyed a different status to those who wrote for the public playhouses. With children's companies, the actors were schoolboys and the writers were in charge. This appealed to the university-educated playwrights who came to the fore in the late 16th century, including Christopher Marlowe. The success of the children's companies may be explained by the way "their puppet-like, stylised performance appropriately lowered the spectator's defence". (Styan) Shakespeare refers to these children's companies in *Hamlet* (1601) when Rosencrantz tells Hamlet of "an eyrie of children, little eyases, that cry out on the top of question and are most tyrannically clapped for't..." The quarrels between playwrights, the so-called War of the Theatres, were conducted through their plays. Rosencrantz reports that "many wearing rapiers are afraid of goosequills".

## CHIROMANCY

The practice of foretelling events and discovering hidden matters by studying the hand – 'chiro' is Greek for hand.

## COLERIDGE, S T

"In Ben Jonson you have an intense and burning art..." (*Table Talk*)

## COSTUMES

It wasn't until the late 18th century that an audience expected actors to be dressed in period costumes. (Thomas)

## CRIME

The London underworld was highly organised, with division of labour, demarcation of areas of activity, rapid disposal of stolen goods and systematic training of recruits. (Salgãdo) Criminals acquired an impressive variety of skills. They were fortune tellers, cutpurses, pickpockets, confidence tricksters and forgers. They would often team up in groups or pairs, one acting as a decoy or "circling boy", to work the taverns, bowling alleys, baiting rings, theatres, brothels and gambling dens. Prostitutes worked closely with criminals or "crossbiters". Crime in London was seasonal: theft rose between late autumn and early spring when times were hardest and nights were longest. In contrast to the businesslike criminal mindset, the law officers were disorganised, inefficient and lacklustre.

## DAGGER, THE

A pub in Holborn, then well-known for pies and gambling, where Face meets the lawyer's clerk, Dapper. London was awash with pubs. The Swiss tourist Thomas Platter wrote, "I have never seen more taverns and ale-houses in my whole life than in London." There were three main classes of pubs: an 'ordinary' was a tavern. An alehouse was more comfortable, often superior to the comfort of people's own homes. An inn offered overnight accommodation. After the Reformation, pubs had grown more popular for two reasons. One, traditional types of popular entertainment (sports events, religious festivals) had declined. Two, the shift from ale to beer had led to the demise of home-brewing. Beer lasted longer and tasted better.

## DEE, JOHN

A possible model for Subtle, Dr John Dee was an astrologer, mathematician, alchemist and adviser to Queen Elizabeth. The Queen's favourite, the Earl of Leicester, asked Dr Dee to consult the stars to fix the right day for the coronation of Queen Elizabeth. The gossip John Aubrey wrote about Dee, "He used to distill egg-shells and 'twas from hence that Ben Jonson had his hint of *The Alchemist*, whom he meant." Others have taken John Dee and his world more seriously. The groundbreaking scholarship of Frances Yates in the 1960s restored Dee to the prestige of a "Renaissance magus". While a student at Cambridge, Dee had studied 18 hours a day. His library of 3,000 books was more complete in its field than either Oxford or Cambridge. The poet laureate Ted Hughes described Dee as "the most celebrated English philosopher of the day: a man of prestige and influence. His Occult Neoplatonism was…moving towards a deepening preoccupation with the conjuration of spirits and angels that eventually almost swallowed him up."

## DICKENS, CHARLES

More than 200 years later, Dickens displayed (at least) three of Jonson's most distinctive qualities: a delight in London types, a gift for caricature and a matchless ear for idiom. In 1845 a group of amateur actors, several of whom wrote for *Punch*, performed Jonson's *Every Man In His Humour*. Dickens played Bobadil, the boastful soldier (a Falstaffian type). His performance (said biographer John Forster) was a "picture of bombastical extravagance and comic exaltation". Harold Pinter shares Jonson's interest in the idioms of London speech and (like Jonson) writes characters who don't listen to what each other says.

## DONNE, JOHN

Poet and friend of Jonson's, with a keen interest in alchemy. In poems like the 'Nocturnal Upon St Lucy's Day', 'Love's Alchemy' and 'Love's Growth', Donne uses alchemical imagery. In 'The Sun Rising', he uses alchemy as an example of falsehood. Compared to the life of the poet who is in love, "All honour's mimic; all wealth alchemy." In 'Love's Alchemy' Donne compares the chemist's failure to find the Philosopher's Stone with unrequited love:

And as no chymique yet th'Elixar got…
So, lovers dream a rich and long delight,
But get a winter-seeming summers night.

## DREAMS

Jacobeans were strongly influenced by their dreams. In 1628 the essayist Owen Feltham wrote, "in sleep we have the naked and natural thoughts of our souls." The successful Virginian colonist John Rolfe married the Indian maiden Pocahontas after a dream told him to get on with it.

## EXCHANGE, THE

In 1609 Sir Robert Cecil set up England's first shopping mall, The Exchange.

## FAIRY QUEEN, THE

Jonson had real life examples for the Fairy Queen subplot in *The Alchemist*. Two Jacobean fraudsters, Alice and John West, claimed that they were the King and Queen of the Fairies and could bring money and happiness to whoever they wished. Evidence at the trial revealed how they had conned Mr and Mrs Thomas Moores, by taking the couple into a vault, showing them two people dressed like the King and Queen of the Fairies and bags marked "This is for Thomas Moores" and "This is for his wife". Neither Mr nor Mrs Moores was allowed to touch the bags. Alice and John West were found guilty and sent to the pillory. Jonson used the story of another fraudster, John Darrall, a Puritan preacher and fake exorcist, in *The Devil Is An Ass*. Darrall made his accomplice swallow black lead to cause foaming at the mouth during the fake exorcism.

## FATHER–SON RELATIONSHIPS

The additions that Jonson made to Thomas Kyd's highly successful 1580s play *The Spanish Tragedy* concentrate on the theme of fatherhood and the difficulty of coming to terms with the death of a child. Jonson responded with what for the 16th and 17th centuries was "abnormal intensity" to the deaths of children. (Barton)

## FAUSTUS, DR

Marlowe's version of Faust was a key figure of the age: the scholar who had gone too far. Faustus says that only magic "will resolve me of all ambiguities". The discarding of traditional scholarship in favour of occult studies was a path followed by Giordano Bruno, Simon Forman, Dr John Dee and others. Shakespeare's Prospero in *The Tempest* (1611) was a late addition to the ranks of the scholar-magician. Faustus is Latin for luck or prosperity; Prospero is Italian for luck or prosperity.

## FEMALE CHARACTERS

There were no women actors. Female characters were played by boys.

## FENG SHUI

In *StageWrite*, the playwright Samuel Adamson compares Drugger's concerns about the layout of his shop to feng shui. Like alchemy, feng shui has an ancient and elaborate history and is bedevilled by phoneys.

## FIRE

Except for the plague, the biggest threat facing Londoners was fire. (In 1665, London was devastated by the first; in 1666, by the second.) Most fire-fighting tools were primitive, limited largely to leather buckets, ladders and large hooks, which were used to tear down timbers and thatch before sparks could spread. Fire-fighting inventions included the hand-squirt (introduced in the 1590s) and the manual fire-engine (introduced in 1625).

## FLAMEL, NICOLAS

14th century French alchemist whose mysterious wealth enabled him to leave enough money to found 14 hospitals, build three chapels and endow seven churches (Marshall); *also* alchemist and opera-lover; lives in Devon with wife, Perenelle. Sole current possessor of the Philosopher's Stone and friend of Professor Dumbledore. (Rowling)

## FLOWERS

Along the Thames there were spacious gardens, flower beds and fruit trees. Wild radishes grew in the stone walls. Foxgloves grew in Piccadilly ditches. Where the National Theatre stands, there were watercress beds. Chelsea was rural England. Trees densely covered the hills of Hampstead.

## FOOD

Most people lacked Vitamin A (vegetables) and Vitamin D (milk and eggs). The upper-classes didn't believe in fresh vegetables. Anyone who could afford meat, ate a great deal of it. "We...eat more meat at one meal," wrote the playwright Thomas Nashe, "than the Spaniard or Italian do in a month." It was a diet that led to constipation. Before a big lunch, guests might be served sliced radishes dipped in salt, oysters, or salt beef with mustard. The main course might be chicken, bacon, goose, pig, roast beef, roast veal, lamb, capons, rabbit, venison, quail and larks. The pudding might be tart, gingerbread, fritters, cheese, jellies or fruit.

## FOOTBALL

An early match report appears in *The Anatomie of Abuses*. The Puritan Philip Stubbes wrote: "sometimes their necks are broken, sometimes their backs, sometimes their legs, sometime their arms, sometime one part thrust out of joint, sometime another, sometime their noses gush out with blood, sometime their eyes start out..."

## GAMBLING

The occupation of a gamester, playboy or rake, eg: Surly in *The Alchemist* and Tom Quarlous in *Bartholomew Fair*. Gamesters gambled on cards, dice, horses, foot-races, bear-baiting and cock-fighting.

## GIBBERISH

The great Arab alchemist Jabir ibn Hayyan was known in Latin as Geber (with a soft G). His writings were considered impossible to understand and gave rise to the word 'gibberish'.

## HENRY, PRINCE

The year *The Alchemist* opened, the investiture took place of Henry, Prince of Wales. He was the country's future. The grandson of Mary, Queen of Scots, great-grandson of Henry VIII, his emergence as a national figure was greeted with a surge of Tudor sentiment. Henry was a theatre buff like his mother Queen Anne. He was patron of the Prince's Men, led by Henslowe's son-in-law Edward Alleyn. He was also a patron to Jonson. It was a matter of status to be patron of a company of actors. The Stuarts were using the arts as a branch of politics and Henry's household, set up after he had arrived in England, became a centre of opposition to the policies of King James. Henry died in 1612. It was rumoured he had been poisoned by his father, James I, who was jealous of his success.

## HERBS

Herbs were considered one of the main protections against the plague. Quarantine was the other. Francis Herring, Doctor in Physicke, published this advice in 1603: "Let men in their private houses amend the air by laying in their windows sweet herbs as marjoram, thyme, rosemary, balm, fennel, peniroyal, mints, etc. Likewise by burning juniper, thyme, bay leaves, cloves, cinnamon... the poorer may burn wormwood, rue, thyme..." (Lee)

## HOT AIR

Sir Epicure calls Face a "fire-drake", "Lungs", "Puff" and "Zephyrus". (A fire-drake was a dragon; Zephyrus was god of the west wind.) "Wind, plume, puff, perfume, mist, vapor, steam, smoke, fume, fart – such words return throughout *The Alchemist*," writes Ian Donaldson, "hinting at the imminent vaporisation of wealth, language, and personality itself". (*Casebook*)

## HUMOURS

The theory of humours is that there are four elements in life – fire, air, water and earth – and these are matched in human terms by four humours: blood, phlegm, choler and bile. Each person is dominated by one of these humours. A common treatment for illness was to rebalance the humours by blood-letting.

## ILLNESS

Since there were no antiobiotics, an illness had to run its course. "Stuart Englishmen were, by our standards, exceedingly liable to pain, sickness and premature death." Many of the beliefs in this period stemmed from this "helplessness in the face of disease". (Thomas)

## IMMIGRANTS

There were more burials than births in London. The reason that the population kept growing was the influx of immigrants. A Dutchman living in London said, "the most toilsome, difficult and skilful works are chiefly performed by foreigners".

## INFANT MORTALITY

The rates of infant mortality were high: 30% of babies didn't survive to their first birthday; 50% of children didn't survive to their fifth birthday.

## JAMES I, KING

James had been King of England for seven years when *The Alchemist* opened. His mother was Mary, Queen of Scots, and his father was Lord Darnley. In 1589, James married Anne of Denmark. (He was 23, she was 15.) James was intellectual, bisexual and passionate about hunting. It's thought he spent half his waking life on the hunting field. James was also the most prolific author the English monarchy has had. A believer in divine right, James led a court deemed "corrupt without style". James did not "choose men for his jobs but bestowed jobs on his men". (Trevor-Roper, quoted in Kenyon) Sexual favours were exchanged for appointments. Magicians and their black arts were employed to influence affairs.

## JARGON

The link between the jargon used by Puritans and the jargon used by alchemists is made explicit in *Volpone* when Volpone, disguised as a quack doctor, sells his wares to the crowd. One of those listening to his bogus patter says it has no parallel "but Alchimy...or Broughton's books". Hugh Broughton was the Puritan author of *A Concent of Scripture*, which Jonson plundered as material for Dol Common's Biblical ravings.

## JUNG, CARL GUSTAV

In alchemy Jung found a system of symbols that helped define his ideas about archetypes, the collective unconscious and the process of internal growth, which he termed individuation. "Only after I had familiarised myself with alchemy did I realise that the unconscious is a *process*..." At first he thought alchemical texts were "blatant nonsense", but later decided they were the "historical counterparts to the psychology of the unconscious". He believed modern dreams were full of alchemical symbolism (eg: rose, eagle, king and queen, fiery dragons). The movement in alchemy from disintegration to purification and reintegration closely paralleled his understanding of the process of psychological development. From 1947 Jung worked with the Nobel prize-winning physicist Wolfgang Pauli on publicising (in Pauli's words) "the collision in the 17th century between the magic-alchemistic and scientific ways of thinking". Jung also believed that alchemists were working through their unconscious. "In a manner broadly comparable to the relationship of a painter to the colours and materials of his palette and studio, the alchemist projected psychological associations, of which he was neither fully conscious nor in full control, into the metals, retorts, and other materials of his laboratory." (Campbell)

## KELLEY, EDWARD

Assistant to Dr John Dee, acting as his 'skryer' or crystal-gazer. Together they held seances in which they claimed to be in touch with angels. "The seances came to an end when one of the angels suggested wife-swapping." (Martin) Kelley's most successful alchemical experiment was "the transformation of himself – from committed felon to one of the most sought after adepts of the age". (Marshall)

## LANGUAGE

Precise use of language lies at the heart of Jonson's moral vision of the world. He was the author of a book on English grammar. "Language most shows a man," he wrote, "Speak that I may see thee." He also wrote: "Wheresoever manners and fashions are corrupted, language is. It imitates the public riot." One of the features of the Reformation had been an antipathy towards images (seen in the Dissolution of the Monasteries) and a new respect for the written word. Iconoclasm, the smashing of images, returned with the Civil War. The King James version of the Gospel of St John opens: "In the beginning was the Word..."

## LIFE EXPECTANCY

A person's life expectancy in Jonson's time was 32 years: 30 to 35 years in wealthier parts of London, 20 to 25 years in the poorer parts. Many prosperous men survived until their 50s. Forty was considered the beginning of old age. Almost a third of the population of four million was under the age of 15.

## LONDON

By 1610 London was the largest city in Europe. Two hundred years before, London hadn't even been in the top ten European cities. The city's growth had been powered by trade, which had led to an increase in population, a boom in new buildings and (finally) a flourishing of the arts. London was unusual because it was (a) the major trading city in the country and (b) its political and legal centre. London was ten times as big as its nearest English rivals, Bristol and Norwich. Seven gates led into the city of London: Moorgate, Bishopsgate, Ludgate, Aldgate, Aldersgate, Cripplegate, Newgate. At night-time these huge city gates were closed. (The gates were demolished in the 18th century.) The main thoroughfare between the cities of London and Westminster was the Strand. London also boasted the most extensive river frontage. The wall that defended the riverside gave way to wharves, warehouses, quays. "London was more of an agglutination than any kind of classical construction, buildings stuck together and clotted as a mass of swallows' or bats' nests." (Nicolson) London ended at Clerkenwell. The freshest milk could be obtained from a dairy farm immediately north of the city walls.

## LOW COUNTRIES, THE

The Dutch were involved in two wars: one against the Spanish; the other against the sea. A good deal of the Low Countries (what is now Belgium, Luxembourg and the Netherlands) lies beneath the level of the North Sea. Floods could be as devastating as the plague, killing tens of thousands. In 1609, the year before *The Alchemist*, the Dutch and the Spanish signed a Twelve Year Truce with the north becoming Protestant and the south becoming Catholic. For the Dutch, freedom and independence was (by definition) anti-Spanish and anti-Catholic. As a young man, Jonson had fought in the Netherlands against the Spanish. The great trade centres of the Low Countries enjoyed what Dr John Dee called "the intertraffic of the mind". The Low Countries were also populated with English spies monitoring the spread of Spanish influence. "Radical Protestantism poured in from Germany, Renaissance science and art from Italy, news of navigational discoveries from Portugal, and imperial forces from Spain." (Woolley)

## MAGIC

Magic and science, like alchemy and science, had originally progressed alongside one another, but Protestantism was hostile to the practice of magic. The development of science, along with the increasing number of people who lived in cities, hastened the decline of magic. The anthropologist Bronislaw Malinowski offers this clear distinction: "religion refers to the fundamental issues of human existence while magic always turns round specific, concrete and detailed problems."

## MALCONTENTS

An increasing number of men, educated at Oxford and Cambridge, arrived in London to find there was no employment. They were the Angry Young Men of their time. These malcontents turned their talents to writing city comedies and satires on London life. In *Every Man Out Of His Humour* Jonson hits out at many of the malcontent's favourite targets, "the grain hoarder, the vainglorious knight, the uxorious merchant, the coquettish city wife, the foppish courtier, the affected court lady". (Riggs) John Marston wrote a play *The Malcontent* (1603) and dedicated it to Jonson, his old rival.

## MARRIAGE

Jonson was married at the age of 22. The average age of a bridegroom in this period was 26 plus. Generally, men married late, when they had enough money to set up home; women married young. A woman might be pregnant when she married, but marriage was often seen as dating from the moment of betrothal. When a woman married, her father passed responsibility for his daughter over to the husband. The only women who were not treated as chattels were widows. "Sir, there is lodged, hard by me, A rich young widow..." [II.vi]

## MASQUE

These spectacular entertainments were devised to celebrate special occasions at court. Masques reached the peak of their popularity in the Jacobean age when the most successful ones were created by Jonson in collaboration with the designer Inigo Jones. Jonson wrote his first in 1605, his last in 1625. He averaged about one a year. In 1609 a series of lavish entertainments was staged for the investiture of Henry, Prince of Wales. Jonson also invented the grotesque comic interlude, the anti-masque.

## MASTER-SERVANT RELATIONSHIPS

The comic situation of master and servant (and who exactly is in charge) runs from Plautus's servant Tranio in *Mostellaria* through to Bernard Shaw's chauffeur Henry Straker in *Man and Superman*, J M Barrie's butler in *The Admirable Crichton*, P G Wodehouse's butler in *Jeeves and Wooster* and Antony Jay's civil servant in *Yes, Minister*. In *Every Man In His Humour* the servant Brainworm tries one trick too many and confesses: "I have made a fair mash of it."

## MEAT

Not even butchers could eat meat during Lent.

## MEMORY

The art of memory was developed in the classical period to a highly sophisticated degree. Memory was one of the six branches of oratory. The Greeks considered Mnemosyne to be the mother of the muses. Jacobean culture still valued techniques of memory, which often involved topographical devices, or memory maps, in which the mental image of a house was constructed (for instance) and complex ideas were stored in separate rooms. Visualisation was central to memory as sight was considered the strongest of the senses.

## MOCK ENCOMIUM

This classical device appealed to Jonson (and to Erasmus in *Praise of Folly*). The mock encomium praises things that are unworthy of praise. This way, the writer has no need to state his own position as the characters condemn themselves out of their own mouths. Jonson uses the device in the opening moment of *Volpone*, when Volpone is lying in his large bed and, as he awakes, he lavishes praise on his gold. "Good morning to the day; and next, my gold! Open the shrine, that I may see my saint."

## MONEY

A penny was 1d. A 'groat' was 4d. A 'crown' was five shillings. An 'angel' was 10 shillings. A 'rose noble' was 15 shillings. A 'sovereign' was 20 shillings. Foreign coins in circulation included French crowns, Spanish ducats and Dutch florins.

1d (a penny) would buy a loaf of bread or admission to the playhouse as a groundling;

3d would buy a pipe of tobacco;

6d would buy a bag of nuts at the playhouse;

7d was the pay of an unskilled labourer (in 1560);

8d would buy two dozen eggs;

One shilling (1s) would buy a poor man shoes;

1s 2d would pay a skilled tradesman for a day;

7s would hire a horse for a week;

8s would buy a pair of fashionable boots;

£3 would be the annual wage of a maidservant;

£15 the annual salary of a grammar school master;

£9535 would pay for the annual expenditure on Queen Elizabeth's wardrobe. (Picard)

## MORALITY PLAY

*The Alchemist* has similarities to the old-fashioned morality play in which a trio of Vice figures seduce gullible mankind away from the path of righteousness. Face, Dol Common and Subtle here represent the world, the flesh and the devil, offering people fantasy versions of themselves.

## NAMES

The Archbishop of Canterbury, Richard Bancroft, complained about the Puritan habit of calling children names like 'The Lord-is-near', 'More-trial', 'Reformation', 'Morefruit' and 'Dust'. The same complaint is made in *The Alchemist*: "Nor call yourselves by names of Tribulation, Persecution, Restraint, Long-patience, and such-like..." There were children in Sussex called 'Eschew-Evil', 'Lament', 'Sorry-for-sin', 'Faint-not', 'Give-thanks' and 'Sin-deny'. Benjamin was not a common Christian name in 16th century England. English surnames were still a relatively new development. Jonson's surname changed from Johnson to Jonson and may originally have been the Scots version, Johnstone. The word "name" also referred to reputation. About 75% of London's tradesmen and artisans could sign their name.

## NECROMANCY

The art of telling the future by communication with the dead.

## NEWNESS

"Goods were pouring into England," writes Adam Nicolson, "silks, lace, Venetian glass, tin-glazed ceramics, fine thick Italian paper, German swords and armour, Turkish carpets and Venetian instruments, metal-threaded textiles..." Sir Epicure catches this baroque pleasure in material objects. "My shirts I'll have of taffeta-sarsnet, soft and light as cobwebs..."

## NEWS

It did not become common until the 16th century to imply that events were unprecedented or that they were 'news'. This represented the replacement of a cyclical view of history with a linear one. (Thomas) Printed news-sheets began in the early 17th century. Originality had yet to become a virtue that would be praised by literary critics.

## NEWTON, ISAAC

The 20th century economist John Maynard Keynes acquired Newton's papers and was amazed to discover how much time Newton had devoted to alchemy. Keynes said Newton was "not the first of the Age of Reason; he was the last of the magicians..." In his day, Newton had the largest collection of books on alchemy. His rooms in Cambridge were decorated in crimson: the final stage of the alchemical process is symbolised by the colour red. Newton wrote "alchemy does not trade with metals as ignorant vulgars think..." He believed "they who search after the Philosopher's Stone [are] by their own rules obliged to a strict and religious life".

## NEW WORDS

The English language was expanding rapidly. New words coined in the early 1600s include: 'factory' and 'undergrowth' (1600), 'commandingly' (1603), 'assassination' (1606), 'invidious' (1606), 'bayonet' (1611), 'briny' (1612) and 'immaturely' (1620).

## 'OFFICE, THE'

The playwright Samuel Adamson compares Jonson's humour with Ricky Gervais's; in both, a character's own remarks reveal the depth of their vanity and self-deception.

## ORACLES

Clients might be sceptical of a particular oracle, but never of oracles in general. They seldom pooled their experience. There was no consumer testing. (Thomas)

## PARLIAMENT

Only called when King James wanted to address it. There was no government in the modern sense. There was no prime minister, no cabinet.

## PIE-CORNER

Near Smithfield, where many cooks had shops. Jeremy meets Subtle here, hungrily snuffing up his meal of steam because he cannot afford to eat.

## PLAGUE

No one in Jonson's time knew what caused the plague. Doctors could do little more than recommend inhaling herbal aromas – marjoram, thyme, fennel, rosemary, mint – to combat the poisonous air. For the Puritans, of course, there was a simple answer to what was happening. "The causes of plagues are sin...and the causes of sin are plays." The plague struck London badly in 1592–93 and again in 1603 and in 1609. (The Great Plague of London was 1665.) The plague made the rich flee the city and forced the playhouses to close down. Once the death rate reached a certain level any activity that brought large groups of people together was considered dangerous. A plague season was terrible news for theatres. When Sir Epicure says that he will fright the plague out of the kingdom, Surly says "the players will sing your praises then". The closure of the London theatres meant that *The Alchemist* had its first performance in Oxford. During the plague, citizens were compelled to burn their rubbish three times a week. The effective introduction of quarantine measures probably played a decisive part in eradicating the disease in Europe. It wasn't until 1894, during an epidemic in Hong Kong, that the plague bacillus was isolated and the disease first understood. The disease is spread by the bite of a rat's flea, which feeds on the blood of an infected rat. The bacilli that have been ingested by the flea multiply inside the flea till they block the entrance to its stomach. If the flea moves from feeding off a rat to feeding off a human, the human's blood is ingested and immediately regurgitated (the flea's stomach is blocked) and the plague bacilli enter the human bloodstream. The first sign would be a soft black swelling in the neck, groin or armpit (hence the name Black Death). This was followed by headaches and delirium. The plague claimed two-thirds of those it infected, most dying within two or three days. After the Great Plague, there were no further outbreaks in this country. Recent research, however, suggests that the rat's flea was not the only carrier of a disease which claimed so many lives so rapidly. The plague may also have spread through a waterborne intestinal disease. The plague still exists in parts of Asia and also in some western areas of the United States, where it is spread by squirrels, prairie dogs, chipmunks and family pets that have been infected.

## PLAUTUS

One of only two writers of Roman comedy whose work has survived. (The other is Terence.) Jonson uses the plot of Plautus' *Mostellaria* for *The Alchemist*. In Mostellaria the master leaves the house empty and the servant and an accomplice take it over. Jonson first considered Plautus's work for adaptation when he attempted a comedy partly based on *Amphitryo*, which involves two sets of identical characters. Jonson abandoned the idea because he thought it would not be possible to find actors who resembled each other closely enough for it to convince an audience. Shakespeare wasn't at all troubled by this, and borrowed the plot for *The Comedy of Errors*. In *The Case is Altered* Jonson borrowed his main plot from Plautus's *The Captives* and his sub-plot from the same author's *Pot of Gold*. Here, the main focus is on the father-son relationship.

## PLAY LENGTH

The average length of a play was between 2,500 and 3,000 lines. At a very rough estimate, 1,000 lines runs about an hour. *Bartholomew Fair* is 4,200 lines long, which is matched only by *Hamlet*.

## PLAYWRIGHT

When Jonson began his career as a playwright he took up a profession that didn't exist when he was born. Christopher Marlowe and Shakespeare were eight years older than Jonson. Along with their contemporaries, John Marston, Thomas Dekker, and Thomas Heywood, they created a new job. Heywood claimed that he had had "an entire hand, or at the least a main finger" in 220 plays. Henslowe paid his writers, or team of writers, an average of £6 for a new script. Jonson had high-minded reservations about becoming a full-time playwright. He preferred to be a gentleman who wrote for the stage. Jonson even employed the word 'playwright' as a term of abuse. He wanted his plays to be considered as literature and to be printed and read at leisure. In 1616 Jonson published a collection of his plays, poems and masques titled *The Workes of Benjamin Jonson*. He was widely mocked at the time for doing so. Jonson believed the playwright's task was to:

> Speak of the intents,
> The counsels, actions, orders and events
> Of state, and censure them.

## POPULATION
There were about four million people in the whole country. Ninety per cent of them lived in the countryside. Nearly half the population was under 25. London had a population of nearly 200,000, and rising fast. The population grew, not because Londoners were overcoming disease or the dangers of childbirth, but as a result of the constant stream of immigrants.

## PROJECTION
A term for the final stage in the alchemical process. It was applied to espionage: a "projector" was an agent who provoked suspects into revealing themselves as spies. In *The Reckoning* Charles Nicholl connects Christopher Marlowe's role as a projector with his murder in Deptford.

## PROSTITUTE
The Inuit people have a great many names for snow. Jacobean Londoners had a great many names for prostitute: 'guinea-bird', 'punk', 'bawd', 'harlot', 'plover', 'quail', 'whore', 'trug', 'stale', 'callet' and 'Winchester goose'. This last one referred to the Bishop of Winchester, in whose diocese of Southwark so many prostitutes worked.

## PURITANS
One of Jonson's main targets was Puritans, who saw public playhouses as places of sexual licence and agitated to have them closed down. Jonson shared this preoccupation with Shakespeare (Malvolio in *Twelfth*

*Night*; Angelo in *Measure for Measure*). In Jonson's *Bartholomew Fair*, Rabbi Zeal-of-the-Land Busy, an elder and prophet of 'the Brethren', is a kill-joy on a grand scale. He dislikes long hair because it is "an ensign of pride". He dislikes ale because it is "a drink of Satan's". He dislikes the smoke of tobacco because it keeps us "in mist and error". Most of all, he dislikes the temptations of "fleshly woman". In 1604, the year after James I became king, he held a conference at Hampton Court to hammer out a religious settlement. (At this conference the decision was taken to commission the King James Version of the Bible.) James I believed in the divine right of kings and had no tolerance for religious sects and separatists, who did not even believe in the authority of bishops. Puritan clergy were excommunicated for non-conformity after the Hampton Court Conference and many moved to Holland, and later to America. The Puritans in *The Alchemist* and *Bartholomew Fair* may be comic creations but the impact Puritans had on English life was immense. "Their voices were heard more and more throughout the land, rising from a rumble to a roar till, 30 years later, with the outbreak of the Civil War, and the ensuing victory of the Puritans, Rabbi Busy's prophesy of destruction came true. Then, for a time, the noise of the Fair would be stilled..." (Salgãdo) For better and worse, Puritanism shaped the modern world. The Pilgrim Fathers who left England on the Mayflower in 1620 founded a country that 400 years later is still deeply religious.

## ROMANTIC COMEDY

In *Every Man Out Of His Humour* Jonson attacks Shakespeare's style of romantic comedy. "Romantic Comedy begins with wretchedness and the threat of danger but ends happily. Satiric Comedy teaches by exposing the errors of city folk." (Jamieson, quoting Nevill Coghill)

## RUDOLPH II

The Holy Roman Emperor was a manic depressive with an obsession for collecting. He lived in Prague Castle, a town within a town, to which he drew many of the great astrologers, alchemists, mathematicians and artists of the age. "As with all serious alchemists, he considered the discovery of the Philosopher's Stone to be an outer sign of inner enlightenment which could lead to the immortality of the soul." (Marshall) Rudolph died in 1612, two years after *The Alchemist* opened.

## SABBATH

The Puritans advocated six days' work a week with the Sabbath a day of rest. The earlier, more medieval, idea of work had been to do the amount that was required (eg: to get the harvest in) and then not do any more.

## ST PAUL'S

The cathedral of St Paul's dwarfed the surrounding city: this was the pre-Christopher Wren version. The aisle in the centre of the Cathedral, called Paul's Walk, resembled a forum or market-place, thronged with lawyers, servants in search of work, men about town and thieves. St Paul's was at the very heart of life in the city.

## SEPARATISTS

The Separatists were a group of Puritans who had moved from England to Holland. They were 'silent Saints' because, as dissenters, they were not allowed to preach in England. Rabbi Zeal-of-the-Land Busy is glad to be "separated from the heathen of the land, and put apart in the stocks for the holy cause".

## SLEEP

The importance of sleep in Jacobean life is shown by the high value Jacobeans attached to beds, usually the most expensive item of domestic furniture. Beds had developed from straw pallets on earthen floors to wooden frames with pillows, sheets, blankets and covers. Sir Epicure says, "I will have all my beds blown up, not stuffed; Down is too hard."

## SOUTHWARK

Noted for its playhouses, bear and bull rings, brothels and five prisons – the Clink, the Compter, the King's Bench, the Marshalsea and the White Lyon.

## SPAIN

The USA became embroiled in Vietnam because of the 'domino theory': that is, if one country fell to communism, the country next door would fall soon after, like a row of dominoes. In Elizabethan England, the Secretary of State, Sir Francis Walsingham, subscribed to a version of the domino theory: England had to stop the mighty advance of Spain in Europe. (Nicholl) The sequence of events was this: in 1576, Antwerp had been laid waste by the Spanish. In 1585 Elizabeth committed

England to military intervention in the Low Countries. In 1587 the execution of Mary Queen of Scots and Drake's raid on Cadiz compelled the Spanish to attack England. In 1588 the English defeated the Spanish Armada. (This is why Dame Pliant, who would not have been alive that year, says: "Never sin' eighty-eight could I abide them.") In 1598, the Spanish-French peace treaty increased the chance that England and Spain would go to war together. In 1601 Spanish troops landed in Ireland and were routed. In 1604 England and Spain made peace. It is argued (broadly) that the Spanish were locked into an old feudal model of nobility and peasants, and failed to create a prosperous middle class. This led, in particular, to an inefficient and class-bound navy. The Spanish aristocrats' love of chivalry and splendour (caught by Surly in his performance as the Spanish Don) was out-of-step with the modern world rapidly developing in Northern Europe. The novelist Cervantes witnessed Spain's imperial triumphs and defeats. In 1605 he published Part One of *Don Quixote*, which features the lofty and ineffectual knight errant and his squire Sancho Panza; in 1615 he published Part Two.

## STDs
The pox, or VD, was one of several diseases marked by pustular eruptions of skin. For the Puritan, venereal disease was a sign that God was punishing the sin.

## STREETS
Mostly they were narrow, crowded, rowdy, smelly and dangerous. Men carried swords in the street. There were carcasses, dunghills, and piles of rubbish. The only streets, which we might recognise as such, were Cheapside and the Strand. There was no public lighting. At night, urine and excrement were thrown out of windows and doors as 'piss-pots' were emptied. Defecation in public was common.

## TABLE MANNERS
It was important to wash your fingers and make sure your neighbour's fingers had also been washed.

## TAXI
You could hail a water-taxi from the stairs at Blackfriars. ("Eastward ho!", "Westward ho!")

## THAMES, RIVER

Fish still swam in shoals. London Bridge was the only bridge spanning the Thames. The high tide could produce a difference in water level of 25 feet. The city controlled the traffic policy on this main transport route.

## THEATRE

The two biggest threats to the theatre were the plague and Puritanism. The plague closed theatres in 1592–94, 1603 and 1609. The Puritan Parliament closed the theatres in 1642. The theatres then stayed closed until the Restoration of Charles II in 1660. When the theatres reopened, they did so as Restoration Theatre. "The King's return to the throne, when it occurred, restored a court that imposed the mid-century tastes of the French court on the literacy and manners of a nation whose radical Englishness it had every reason to fear…the prose of Milton was replaced overnight…by the prose of Addison, which in all essentials is still our cultivated norm." (Hughes)

## THEATREGOERS

Ate apples, pears, nuts; drank ale and wine. Theatre-going was a risky activity. Like the characters in *The Alchemist*, the audience had stayed in London and not fled the plague. Congestion was thought to spread the disease. Whenever the weekly mortality rate reached epidemic proportions theatres were closed down. The two main acting companies based in London averaged 2,500 paying customers a day, 15,000 a week. The total number of London theatregoers was under 40,000. Unlike today, there was a great deal of activity in the audience (eating, drinking, stealing, sex). "Playhouse poultry" were prostitutes looking for clients in the audience. When it came to insulting an audience, no dramatist, not even Bernard Shaw, managed to be as rude as Ben Jonson. (Bamborough)

## TOBACCO

Tobacco arrived in England from America in 1566 and quickly became the new recreational drug. It was expensive enough to be smart: you could go and see three plays for the price of one pipeful of tobacco. The playwright J M Barrie, author of *Peter Pan*, wrote that when Sir Walter Raleigh introduced tobacco to this country "the glorious Elizabethan age began… Men who had hitherto only concerned themselves with the narrow things of home put a pipe into their mouths and became philosophers." King James I was a leading voice against tobacco and wrote his *Counterblast to Tobacco* in 1604: "A custom loathsome to the eye, hateful to the nose, harmful to the brain, dangerous to the lungs." (Louis XIV, Napoleon and Hitler would also demonise tobacco.) Puritans drove home the idea that smoking was a waste of time by quoting Psalm 102: "My days are consumed like smoke". The atheist playwright Christopher Marlowe believed that Holy Communion would be "much better being administered in a tobacco pipe". Shakespeare never mentions tobacco in his plays, but Jonson makes frequent references to it. In *Every Man In His Humour*, the Falstaffian figure, Bobadill, proposes a bunch of radishes and salt "to taste our wine, and a pipe of tobacco to close the orifice of the stomach". In *Every Man Out Of His Humour* Captain Shift offers to teach others how to inhale and exhale, how to progress from the first to the second and third "whiff", and generally how to pass yourself off as a stylish smoker in pubs, playhouses and tilt-yards. Tobacco was a drug that swiftly became an accomplishment. In *Cigarettes Are Sublime* the academic Richard Klein links the modern consciousness that was arising through the spread of printed books, the discovery of the New World, and the development of rational, scientific methods with the popularity of smoking. "The Age of Anxiety gave itself an incomparable and probably indispensable remedy in the form of tobacco." The first time a cigarette is proffered in literature, Klein points out, is in 1847 when the narrator in Prosper Mérimée's most famous story hands a cigarette to Carmen.

## TOBACCONISTS

Like modern coffee shops, tobacconists developed a sophisticated variety of product. The idea was to make tobacco pleasant to taste and to smell as well as to sniff. Flavours included "citron, aniseed, thyme, saffron, lavender, dill, nutmeg, coriander, vinegar, brown beer, mace, fennel, potash, chamomile, prunes and rosemary". (Schama) Colts-foot is a herb that was used to adulterate tobacco. Anyone who smoked was a "tobacconist".

## TRAFFIC OF THE MIND

The phrase was coined by Dr John Dee. One example of this interplay links Galileo to Ben Jonson. In 1609 Galileo hears news that a telescope is being sold in Amsterdam. Two weeks later he presents his own telescope to the Doge in Venice. The news of this discovery is reported back to King James in a letter from Sir Henry Wootton, the English ambassador to Venice. A friend of Ben Jonson's, Wootton is thought to be the model for Sir Politic Would-be in *Volpone*, the English knight whose mind and notebook is filled with "grave affairs of state".

## TRANSFORMATION

"*The Alchemist* is a play about transformation, as it affects not metals, but human beings." (Barton) "Each of the characters is an alchemist attempting to transform himself by means of his particular 'Philosopher's Stone' into some form higher up on the scale of being than the point at which he began." (Kernan)

## TYBURN

Jonson's thumb was branded with the letter T (for Tyburn, where he would have been hanged). Tyburn was on the site of present-day Marble Arch.

## UNITIES

In general, Jonson followed the classical unities of action, time and place, which limited the events in a play to a single location and 24 hours. The idea of the unities also discourages subplots and the mixing of comic and tragic elements. Shakespeare is not a good example: "with its loose and episodic scenic form, its multiple plots, its vertiginous course from tragedy to comedy and back again, its motley assemblages of character, its profligacy of vocabulary and speech idiom, its jumble of verse and prose". (Bate)

## URINE SAMPLE

In 1669 a German alchemist, Hennig Brandt, mixed gold with an extract of urine and discovered phosphorus.

## 'VENTURE TRIPARTITE'

At a seance at his Mortlake house in the early 1580s, John Dee and his assistant Edward Kelley predicted that a young Polish count, Albrecht Laski, would become King of Poland and discover the Philosopher's Stone. Laski was enthralled. The three of them travelled to Poland and stayed on Laski's estates near Kracow. Laski was disappointed that the experiment consumed more gold than it produced. Literary critics have seen these three as a possible inspiration for Jonson's 'venture tripartite' with Dee as Subtle, Kelley as Face and Laski as Dol Common (in the seances he played the part of the angel).

### VINEGAR

The only regular preventive medicine, or prophylactic, against VD was the washing of genitals in vinegar or white wine. (Salgãdo)

### VIOLENCE

"In pre-industrial societies, violence left few realms of daily life unscathed. Wives, children, and servants were flogged, bears baited, cats massacred, and dogs hanged like thieves. Swordsmen duelled, peasants brawled, and witches burned. Quarrels rose quickly to the surface." (Ekirch)

### 'VOLPONE'

Shows that "it is possible for one clever and self-interested rogue, with the help of an accomplice, to live off society's greed, amassing a vast private fortune simply by pretending to be terminally ill and uncertain as to the choice of an heir". (Barton)

### WALKING

People walked. The whole of London, including Westminster and the Southwark river frontage, was "only three miles long and two miles wide". (Picard)

### WITCHCRAFT

Beneath the pieties of official Christianity lay deep belief in demons, spirits and witches. (Salgãdo) Witch-hunts sprang from the grass-roots, not as a result of pressure from those in authority. The witchcraft craze in England did not survive the scientific scepticism of the later 17th century. At least, as far as the law courts were concerned, more stringent standards of proof were demanded.

### WIZARDS

The number of wizards would continue to rise in England until the Civil War and the interregnum. *The Alchemist* was the first in a series of attacks that Jonson made on wizards. The link between wizardry and crime was well known. "Experience shows that very often famous thieves are also wizards," said the German legal scholar Jacobus Andreas Crucius in 1660. There was a steady prosecution of witches in Elizabethan and Jacobean England. In 1602 the Lord Chief Justice of the Common Pleas said: "The land is full of witches, they abound in all places, I have hanged five or six and twenty of them." A L Rowse wrote that far more people were hanged for cutting a purse or stealing a sheep than for witchcraft.

## WRITERS

In Jonson's time, the profession of letters did not exist. Writers were not protected by laws of copyright. The laws that did exist protected printers. For social historians, some of the most useful documents of the period are by Puritans who wrote slavishly detailed accounts of the things they most abhorred.

# Sources

For the A–Z, I have drawn most heavily on books by Anne Barton, Peter Marshall, Adam Nicolson, Liza Picard, David Riggs, Gāmini Salgādo, and Keith Thomas.

Many of the following books and DVDs that were consulted for the A–Z are available via the NT Bookshop *nationaltheatre.org.uk/ bookshop*. The ones that are harder to acquire, other than the *Jonson Casebook*, are by Barton, Riggs and Sherwood Taylor.

RB

WEBSITES

en.wikipedia.org (for "the dozens", Victor Lustig, and Derren Brown)
mckellen.com/stage/alchemist
channel4.com/history/microsites/H/history/plague
bbc.co.uk/drama/hustle
nytimes.com/2006/08/01/science/0lalch
christianvoice.org.uk
antichristianvoice.org.uk
dh.gov.uk (for bird flu)

BOOKS, PLAYS & JOURNALS

Adamson, Samuel, *StageWrite*, the NT's education newsletter
Bair, Deirdre, *Jung* (2004)
Bamborough, J B, *Ben Jonson: Writers and their Work* (1965)
Barton, Anne, *Ben Jonson Dramatist* (1984)
Barzun, Jacques, *From Dawn to Decadence* (2000)
Bate, Jonathan, *The Genius of Shakespeare* (1997)
Bolt, Rodney, *History Play* (2004)
Bond, Edward, *Plays: 3* (1987)
Campbell, Joseph, *The Masks of God: Creative Mythology* (1968)
Curtis, Elton, et al, *Blackadder: The Whole Damn Dynasty* (1998)
Donaldson, Ian, *Oxford Dictionary of National Biography*, entry on Ben Jonson (2004–06)
Donne, John, *Selected Poems* ed. John Hayward (1950)
Ekirch, A Roger, *At Day's Close: A History of Nighttime* (2005)

Erasmus, *Praise of Folly*, trans. Betty Radice (1971)

Gurr, Andrew, *Playgoing in Shakespeare's London* (1987)

Holden, Anthony, *William Shakespeare* (1999)

Holdsworth, R V (ed.), *Jonson Casebook: Every Man In His Humour/ The Alchemist* (1978)

Hughes, Ted, *Winter Pollen* (1994)

Jonson, Ben, *The Alchemist* ed. Elizabeth Cook (1991)
  *Three Comedies* ed. Michael Jamieson (1966)
  *The Complete Poems* ed. George Parfitt (1975)

Jung, C G, *Memories, Dreams, Reflections* (1963)

Kane, Leslie, *David Mamet in Conversation* (2001)

Kenyon, J P, *The Stuarts* (1958)

Kermode, Frank, *The Age of Shakespeare* (2004)

Kernan, Alvin, *Shakespeare, The King's Playwright* (1995)

Klein, Richard, *Cigarettes Are Sublime* (1993)

Lee, Christopher, *1603* (2003)

Littlewood, Joan, *Joan's Book* (1994)

McIntyre, Ian, *Garrick* (1999)

Mamet, David, *The Spanish Prisoner/The Winslow Boy* (1999)

Marshall, Peter, *The Philosopher's Stone* (2001)
  *The Theatre of the World* (2006)

Martin, Sean, *Alchemy and Alchemists* (2001)

Maurer, David W, *The Big Con* (1940)

Micklethwait, John & Wooldridge, Adrian, *The Right Nation* (2004)

Nicholl, Charles, *The Reckoning* (1992)

Nicolson, Adam, *Power and Glory* (2003)

Picard, Liza, *Elizabeth's London* (2003)

Polito, Robert, *Savage Art – A Biography of Jim Thompson* (1995)

Porter, Roy, *London: A Social History* (1994)
  *The Greatest Benefit to Mankind* (1997)

Riggs, David, *Ben Jonson* (1989)

Rowling, J K, *Harry Potter and the Philosopher's Stone* (1997)

Salgādo, Gāmini, *The Elizabethan Underworld* (1977)

Schama, Simon, *The Embarrassment of Riches* (1987)

Schoenbaum, S, *William Shakespeare* (1977)

Shapiro, James, *1599* (2005)

Stone, Lawrence, *The Family, Sex and Marriage in England 1500–1800* (1977)

Styan, J L, *The English Stage* (1996)

Taylor, F Sherwood, *The Alchemists* (1951)

Thomas, Keith, *Religion and the Decline of Magic* (1971)

Thompson, Jim, *The Grifters* (1963)

Trussler, Simon, *Faber Pocket Guide to Elizabethan and Jacobean Drama* (2006)

Wood, Michael, *In Search of Shakespeare* (2003)

Woolley, Benjamin, *The Queen's Conjuror* (2001)

Yates, Frances, *Giordano Bruno and the Hermetic Tradition* (1964) *The Art of Memory* (1966)

DVDs ABOUT CON ARTISTS

*Catch Me If You Can* (2002), dir. Steven Spielberg

*Confidence* (2003), dir. James Foley

*Heist* (2001), dir. David Mamet

*House of Games* (1987), dir. David Mamet

*Lady Eve, The* (1941), dir. Preston Sturges

*Lavender Hill Mob, The* (1951), dir. Charles Crichton

*Matchstick Men* (2003), dir. Ridley Scott

*Ocean's Eleven* (2001), dir. Steven Soderbergh

*Spanish Prisoner, The* (1997), dir. David Mamet

*Sting, The* (1973), dir. George Roy Hill

*Trouble in Paradise* (1932), dir. Ernst Lubitsch

*Usual Suspects, The* (1995), dir. Bryan Singer

CD

*The Alchymist* on 'Handel Water Music', The Academy of Ancient Music, conducted by Christopher Hogwood (Double Decca)

above: Alex Jennings
below: Amit Shah, Simon Russell Beale, Sam Spruell, Alex Jennings and Nicholas Hytner

Lesley Manville

Simon Russell Beale

above: Rehearsing doors business
below: Props

above: Bryan Dick
below: Alex Jennings and Lesley Manville

Elisabeth Dermot Walsh

Nicholas Hytner (left) and members of the company

above: Tristan Beint
below: Amit Shah